D1314334

Finding God in a
Tangled World

Finding God in a Tangled World

Thoughts & Parables

Juris Rubenis
&
Maris Subacs

Translated from the original Latvian by Paul Valliere

PARACLETE PRESS
BREWSTER, MASSACHUSETTS

Finding God in a Tangled World: Thoughts & Parables

2007   First Printing

Text and Illustrations Copyright © 2007 by Juris Rubenis,
    Maris Subacs, and Zvaigzne ABC Publishers
Translation Copyright © 2007 by Paul Richard Valliere

        Library of Congress Cataloging-in-Publication Data
Rubenis, Juris.
  Finding God in a tangled world : thoughts & parables / Juris
  Rubenis, Maris Subacs ; translated by Paul Valliere.
      p. cm.
ISBN-13: 978-1-55725-495-5
ISBN-10: 1-55725-495-8

  1. Christianity–Miscellanea. 2. Christian life. 3. Bible stories.
  I. Subacs, Maris. II. Title.
  BR124.R78 2007
  242–dc22   2006033728

10 9 8 7 6 5 4 3 2 1

Published by Paraclete Press
Brewster, Massachusetts
www.paracletepress.com
Printed in the United States of America

Contents

Juris Rubenis and Maris Subacs are fresh Christian voices from a little known corner of Europe. Juris is the pastor of Martin Luther Church in Riga, Latvia. Maris is a well known graphic artist in the same city. For more than ten years Juris and Maris have been partners in a unique sort of spiritual conversation, producing more than a dozen collections of meditations, thoughts, and parables. Resembling poetry more than prose and rendered unmistakable by Maris's line drawings, these little books are loved by people of all faiths in Latvia.

Why should North Americans listen to voices from Latvia, a small, relatively poor country on the eastern shore of the Baltic Sea adjacent to Russia? The answer is that, while Latvia might be a small country, it has a big story to tell. For fifty years Latvia was part of the Soviet Union. Regaining its independence in 1991, the country has worked hard to remake itself as a democracy, and in 2004 it was admitted to the European Union. Latvia is thus a window on the vast spiritual drama of the Soviet and post-Soviet world—the drama of atheism and religious persecution, of Communism and its collapse, of spiritual rebirth, of the struggle for human rights, political freedom, and a United States of Europe, and yes, of post-Soviet materialism and reckless globalization.

Juris Rubenis came to the Christian faith as a young adult in Soviet Latvia when atheism was still the state religion. Inspired by a courageous pastor, the Rev. Roberts Feldmanis, Juris was ordained to the Lutheran ministry in 1982 at the age of twenty-one. Maris Subacs, a 1988 graduate of the Latvian Academy of Art, also converted to Christianity as a young man, making a leap of faith that carried him to Roman Catholicism from the turbulent "bohemia" he inhabited as a popular young artist in Riga.

Juris achieved national prominence early in his ministry. In 1986 he took an active role in Helsinki-86, the first above-ground human rights organization in Soviet Latvia, and in the following year he helped found Rebirth and Renewal, an association of Latvian Lutheran pastors calling for religious freedom in the Soviet Union. By this time Mikhail Gorbachev was in power in Moscow. The three Baltic republics of Latvia, Lithuania, and Estonia responded enthusiastically to Gorbachev's reforms, but they also made it clear that they were interested in nothing less than complete independence from the Soviet Union. In 1988, independence-minded Popular Front movements were launched in all three Baltic countries. Juris was one of the founders of the Latvian Popular Front.

The next three years were an exhilarating time for the Baltic peoples—a time of mass meetings, inspired journalism, impassioned choral festivals, charismatic oratory, the return of prisoners and exiles, and the recovery of national pride. With his moral clarity and golden tongue, Juris contributed mightily to the "singing revolution" that swept his native land to freedom.

After the restoration of Latvian independence, a political career lay open to Juris. But after a time of wrestling, he decided his vocation lay not in the state but in the church, the place where he discovered the spiritual freedom that grounds all other freedoms. Under his leadership Martin Luther Church has become the largest church in Latvia and one of the most dynamic congregations anywhere in Europe.

As teachers, Rubenis and Subacs focus on elementary spiritual truths. This makes sense in a post-Communist environment where many people have only recently been exposed to religion. But it is also salutary for more experienced audiences. Like all good theologians, our authors know that the elementary truths about God and the world are also the most important. There is something primal about faith, something that bears repeating over and over again. When we listen, we discover new things in a message we thought we knew very well.

Juris's and Maris's teaching tools are thoughts and parables—pithy observations about the world and brief, deceptively simple stories bearing a moral or spiritual lesson. In biblical perspective the two forms are one and the same. Both are included in the Hebrew word *mashal*, a term sometimes translated "proverb," at other times "parable." The point of a mashal in either form is to precipitate a moment of insight into the difference between wisdom and folly, evil and good, falsehood and truth, time and eternity, human beings and God. Jesus was master of the mashal in both its forms.

The mashal teaches us to practice humility in theology. Our authors repeatedly stress the impossibility of capturing theological truths in any sort of system, even a system of church dogma crafted by the most saintly teachers in the world. God is just too big, Jesus too paradoxical. The mashal, attuned more to paradox and symbol than to propositions, is the perfect medium for theological conversation. It is a means of dialogue with the divine that does not let us forget that God is the Ineffable One.

Maris's drawings convey the same message. His people are small, awkward, and obviously incapable of accomplishing great things on their own, yet they are neither hopeless nor helpless. They stand at all times before a gracious presence that empowers them to do what they could not do by themselves, such as getting their bearings in the cosmos, loving their neighbors, building decent communities, and facing death with hope.

As a churchman, Rubenis stands somewhat outside the mainstream of contemporary Eastern European Christianity. The mainstream is religious traditionalism, with a strong emphasis on the authority of the institutional church. This traditionalism cuts across denominational lines and is as powerful in Protestant churches as it is in the Roman Catholic and Orthodox churches in the region. This should come as no surprise, given that the challenge facing Eastern European religious communities today is to rebuild themselves after the ravages of the Communist period. Religious traditionalism is also attractive because it provides a clear alternative to the materialism and moral nihilism of the post-Communist era. But Juris takes a different approach. His preaching of the Gospel is gentler, more humane, and more tolerant of diversity than the message conveyed by many churches in his part of the world.

Juris's collaboration with a Roman Catholic artist is a further expression of independence. Such ecumenism also reflects the culture of Latvia, which has always been an ethnic and religious crossroads. About a third of the population of Latvia is not Latvian at all, but Russian. In the past a large German population played a leading role in the country, leaving a legacy that is still felt in countless ways. The religious geography of Latvia is likewise complex, with Protestant, Catholic, and Russian Orthodox communities flourishing in roughly equal numbers. Historically Latvia has also been a haven for persecuted or marginalized religious minorities, such as Jews, Moravians, and Russian Orthodox Old Believers. With their respect for diversity and love of dialogue, Rubenis and Subacs honor both the past and the promise of Latvian pluralism.

The Gospel according to Rubenis and Subacs is all about discovering God's grace in unexpected places. For North Americans, Latvia can be one of those places. Juris and Maris know very well that their country is inconspicuous on the global scene. But they also know that the spiritual world is a world of reverse perspective, where a small people can be gifted with a big faith and a narrow gate can open onto a vast and wonderful domain. This basic truth cannot be repeated too often in North America, where we tend to be self-absorbed and dangerously unaware of our limits. We would do well to listen to voices from small countries. "Latvia has a prophet's budget—that is to say, a small one," say Rubenis and Subacs, with a smile at the limited resources of their country. This observation applies also to their books. With modesty and good humor, pastor and artist have done nothing less than the work of prophets. They have borne witness to the mystery of Eden, the mystery of the kingdom of God.

Paul Valliere

Translator's Note

The material in this book is drawn from ten separate works by Juris Rubenis and Maris Subacs published in Riga between 1997 and 2006. The selection and arrangement, including the chapter divisions, are the work of the translator in consultation with Juris Rubenis. All translations were made from the original Latvian.

A bibliography of the Latvian sources including page references is available from the translator, Dr. Paul Valliere, McGregor Professor in the Humanities, Butler University, Indianapolis, Indiana 46208 (pvallier@butler. edu).

The translator expresses deep thanks to Juris Rubenis for our twenty years of friendship, to Maris Subacs for preparing original English-language versions of the drawings, and to Karl Rusa of the Irwin Library of Butler University for his invaluable advice on issues of Latvian-English translation.

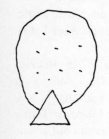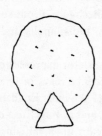

THE GARDEN
WHERE WE WALK
WITH GOD

Eden

One day Adam asked God, "Why am I here?"

"So that I can enjoy your company, and you mine," God replied.

Adam asked, "What can I do to make my joy and yours as great as possible?"

"Just be what I have made you," God said.

Adam replied, "I have heard that the angels think I am disobedient and unholy."

"The angels do not have the feelings for me that you have," God said.

"But I want to be like the angels," Adam said.

"You can't be, you are a human being," God replied.

"The angels seem to know something you do not tell me," Adam said.

"But you understand something the angels do not understand," God explained.

"What is that?" Adam asked.

"What is going on between us when we speak about these things," God replied.

In the beginning we took pleasure in great truths; trivialities came later.

☉

Once there was stillness. It was so profound you could hear God's still and peaceful voice.

☉

Adam said to God, "There is some sort of mystery here in Eden."
"I made it like this so that you can think about Eden forever," God said with a smile.

☉

The truth you deal with must be bigger than you so that you can think about it forever.

☉

In Eden an angel said, "Everything is illusory until you know God."
"Explain that!" the other angels demanded.
"God is the only reason your dreams exist, but God is not a dream. God is who God is."

☉

God created the world.
"Why did you do it?" an angel asked.
"To give you something to think about," God replied.

☉

Once upon a time God created an angel who liked doing the tasks God gave him but who was not a particularly good worker. All the same, God gave him the more important assignments.

"Why didn't you choose a more exemplary worker?" the other angels asked.

"Because this angel cannot live without contact with me," God replied.

In Eden an angel said, "In God there is infinite beauty." All agreed, and for a long time they contemplated God.

There was once a world that came to be called the Garden of Eden. The angels lived there. They were all happy.

"There could not be a better world than this one!" they agreed.

God was silent.

"What do you think of our world?" the angels asked.

"I think it will go bad," God said.

"Why?" the angels asked in surprise.

"Because you will not forgive me if I create something else."

"Why do you need to create something else?"

"Because we want all sorts of things to exist," God replied.

ॐ

God was thinking: "What is to be done? The angel Satan understands us but does not love us. Let us make a new creature who will be able to understand us and love us." So God spoke and created Adam.

ॐ

In Eden an angel said, "Adam does not appreciate the grandeur of God but talks with God as if God were Adam."

ॐ

"I'm chummy with God," Adam announced to the angels one day.
"But God is God!" the angels objected in alarm.
"God seems lonely to me," Adam continued. "God wants someone to be friends with."

ॐ

In Eden an angel said, "Adam is not an ordinary angel."
"He behaves strangely," the others agreed.
"There is supposed to be something of God in him—that's what the Almighty has been heard to say."
"That's funny," the others said. "Adam behaves like a bad angel. He wants to make all his own decisions. Let some good angel have a talk with him."
"Adam, be good!" the holiest angel urged him.
"You mean, I'm not good?" Adam was surprised.
The angel was silent for a moment. "Maybe I shouldn't have said that," he thought.

4

"Of course you are good," he said, "but just try to be more obedient."

In Eden an angel said, "Adam is not as inferior as we think." "What are you saying? Adam is Adam!" the other angels objected, and laughed.
"You'd better not laugh at God!" the angel warned them.

In Eden an angel said, "God loves Adam more than the rest of us because he is not afraid of God."

In Eden one day Adam gathered the angels around him and began explaining what God is like. A respected angel went to see God and asked, "Who is this fellow? Is he a genius or an imposter?"
"He is a creature who has discovered something of God within himself," God explained calmly. "He really does understand something, but of course he is only a creature."

Adam was listening to rock music and tapping his foot. "What are you doing?" the angels asked.
"I am enjoying myself," Adam said, continuing to keep time.
"What a fool!" the angels concluded.
"Oh, you angels!" Adam replied, keeping up the beat.

❧

In Eden an angel said, "The point of the creation of the world is a mystery to us. Only to Adam is it self-evident that he needs a world of his own."

❧

In Eden an angel said, "Adam needs a world of his own because here among us he always feels he is bad."

❧

In Eden an angel said, "Eden will not last forever."
"How can that be?" the others said in alarm.
"We treat Adam badly," the angel replied.
"But Adam is not good!" said the others in surprise.
"There is something of God in him," replied the angel.

❧

Adam was at it again. He was pulling the angels by the wings, and they were indignant.
"I want to study you," Adam explained.
"Shameless!" the angels bristled.
"They're calling me names," Adam complained to God.
"Stop whining," God said. "I'll make you another world."
"And what will it be like there?" Adam asked.
"There you will be able to investigate to your heart's content how everything is put together."
"But how are you put together?" Adam suddenly asked.
"That's rather complicated," God said with a smile.

6

❧

In Eden an angel said, "There are times when Adam wants to be God. He cannot be, so he gets morose."

❧

In Eden an angel said, "Adam wants everyone to treat him like God. If they do not, he becomes unhappy."

❧

Even Adam went to church once a week.

❧

One day Adam said to God, "I need another Adam here in Eden."
"You are wrong," God said. "You need Eve."
"Who is Eve?" Adam asked.
"Someone a little like Adam," God replied.

❧

One day God asked Adam, "Why don't you make friends with any of the animals I have made for you?"
Adam replied, "They do not understand me."
"I understand you," God said, "but you don't want to tell me everything."
"You are so much bigger and stronger than I am," Adam said. "I want someone like myself."
"You will not find anybody who understands you as well as I do," God said to Adam.

7

"I feel lonely," Adam replied. "I am not God. We're just different."
"We are also a bit like each other," God replied.
"I enjoy feeling like God among the animals," Adam said, "but in your presence I feel like one of them."
"I do not know what to say to you," God said. "So I will make another creature like you."
And God created Eve.

One day Adam said to Eve, "I like you!"
"I like you, too," Eve replied.
God laughed and said, "This work of mine has turned out well!"

Adam said to God, "I like Eve very much. I would like a second Eve."
God replied to Adam, "Try to understand the Eve you already have and you won't need another one."

One day Adam said to God, "I want to be like you."
"You already are a bit like me," God said. "You are my image."
"I want to be like the holiest angel."
"Your wish is admirable, but what you really need is Eve," God comforted him.

8

"It is only you I want," Adam said.
"You can see me through Eve," God replied.

 ☙

Adam was hiding from God in the bushes.
"Why have you run away from me?" God asked.
"I have made a terrible discovery. Eve is my real love,
not you," Adam said in tears.
God calmed him down. "Don't worry—in Eve, too, there
is something of me."

 ☙

One day Adam said to God: "I want to be like you."
"That's not possible," God replied, "although there's
nothing bad about your dream."

 ☙

One day Adam asked God: "What will I be like when
you finish making me?"
"Like me," God replied.
"Is that possible?" Adam asked in surprise.
"In one respect, yes, though not in all respects."

 ☙

In Eden there were many kinds of trees. In the middle
grew the tree of life. "Give me something from that
tree," Adam asked God.
"You have to wait," God replied. "Every tree has its
season."

ᔑ

One day Jesus asked his Father, "Why do people say that the forbidden fruit is sweet?"

God replied, "The forbidden fruit has no taste at all. It is neither sweet nor bitter."

"Then why do people want it?" Jesus asked.

"Because they have foolish ideas about Eden," God replied. "They think that disobedience is sweet. But disobedience is utterly tasteless."

ᔑ

In the Garden of Eden there was more than the forbidden fruit.

ᔑ

One angel asked another, "Why does God only walk in the Garden of Eden, not live in it?"

"Because everyone here feels small compared to God," the other angel answered.

ᔑ

The garden of paradise was a place where from time to time Adam could hide from God.

ᔑ

One day Adam said to God, "I am so full of faults. I need someone who can put up with me. I am glad you are like that."

"Oh, my Adam!" God said. "I don't put up with you. I love you."

❧

In Eden an angel said, "The world wants to be wise, but God likes naiveté."
"Explain that!" the other angels asked.
"The world is afraid of being small. It seeks refuge in the illusion of wisdom."

❧

One day Adam asked God, "Why am I so small?"
"Because I am so big," God replied.

❧

One day Adam was looking at the heavens.
"They are so big and wide," he said to God.
"I am the heavens," God replied.
"Don't try to fool me—you are God!" Adam objected.
God breathed a sigh of relief. "Ah, Adam, Adam, you are my beloved child!"

❧

One day Adam asked God, "Why don't you pay me a wage for all the gardening I do here?"
"This is paradise," God said. "Your wages are the beauty you receive from me free of charge."

❧

God loves human beings; the angels do not.

God loves the angels, but there is something they do not quite understand. God loves human beings, but they are wayward.

"How are you?" God asked Adam in Eden one day.
"I'm fine," Adam replied. "But it's awfully quiet around here."
"That is because in me there is peace," God said.
"Satan says that an angel's life is much more interesting. There is always something going on, all sorts of conflicts and wars. What is war?"
"Do not talk with that angel," God rebuked Adam. "He does not wish you well. To be happy, an angel needs one thing, you need something else."

To an angel a foe is a friend.

Human beings, living in the body, can only believe that God exists; the angels can see it.

Theological disputes are quarrels of angels.

Angels are the holiest of God's creatures, but even they have a dark side. Angels err, God does not.

◌

Human beings are not holy the way the angels are, but they are wiser because they bear the image of God.

◌

Angels love human beings when human beings are powerless. They save human beings when human beings are powerful.

◌

Angels reach paradise by way of obedience, human beings by way of freedom—a freedom that has accepted obedience.

◌

Adam complained to God, "The angels are saying bad things about me."
"About me, too," God comforted him.

◌

In Eden an angel said, "It is not possible to defeat God."
"That is not quite right," God said.
"Why not?" the others asked, bewildered.
"God can retreat in certain situations," God explained.
"We do not understand," the angels said.
"For example, God can refrain from destroying you for expressing dangerous ideas."

∂

In Eden an angel said, "It's all Adam's fault. It was for him that an imperfect world was created."
"It's actually your fault," God replied. "You did not accept Adam into your world."

∂

An angel said, "Adam's weak in the head."
"By your logic, so am I," God replied.

∂

In Eden an angel said, "God does not like ruling."
"Explain that!" the others demanded.
"God likes it when creatures are what they are."
"Then why is God always demanding obedience from us?"
"He is teaching us to be," the angel replied.

∂

An angel asked God, "Why do you pay so much attention to Adam?"
"He is my friend," God replied.
"Does he say wiser things than the rest of us?" the angel asked.
"No," God said. "But he tells me more about the everyday problems of creation than any other creature does."

∂

Paradise comes to an end with the thought "I am not good."

૭

One day Jesus asked his Father, "Abba, why did you punish Adam?"

"I did not punish him," God replied. "I created a world for him so that he could find his way back to freedom."

૭

One day Eve said to Adam, "You make me feel righteous, even though I am not."

"I think you are righteous," Adam replied.

"It is the angels who are righteous," Eve said. "To be perfectly honest, I am not."

"Well, since I am like you, I must not be righteous, either," Adam said, and he grew sad.

"The best of the angels is Satan," Adam continued, "but for some reason God has forbidden us to talk with him."

"I like him," Eve said. "He is very holy."

"I, too, want to be holy," Adam observed, and he felt even sadder.

"Let's ask Satan how we can be holy," Eve said.

"You cannot be holy," Satan said. "You are made from the dust of the earth."

"Are we really dust?" Adam and Eve asked God.

God was silent, knowing it was so.

Finally God said, "You will have to live in another world, where angels do not talk and where everyone is just like you."

THE GOLDEN CALF
AND THE HEAVENS

2
The Bible

There was once a certain Pharisee. He was not especially meticulous, but he revered the Law of Moses, so the other Pharisees respected him. One day a prostitute approached him.

"Does God love us?" she asked.

"God loves all people," the Pharisee answered.

"Then why did he throw Adam out of paradise?" the woman asked.

"Where is that written?" the Pharisee asked.

"That's what people say," the woman replied.

"It is written: 'But the Lord God called to the man, Where are you?'" the old Pharisee replied quietly.

"Then it must be Eve that God does not like," the woman said. "She is blamed for everything."

"Where is that written?" the Pharisee asked quietly.

"That's what people say."

"It is written: 'This is now bone of my bones and flesh of my flesh,'" the old Pharisee explained quietly.

"And people say there's a horrible snake in paradise," the woman said.

"It is written that it is very beautiful there," the Pharisee explained quietly.

❧

God created a book of stories about God and humanity. "Why is it so long and hard to understand?" someone asked. "So that people will not think they know all there is to know about God," God replied.

❧

The knowledge of God begins and ends with idols. In between there is the Bible.

❧

Idolatry is the illusion that you can understand God.

❧

Someone asked God, "What is the Bible?"
God replied, "The Bible is a book we have made out of our life together with human beings and human beings' life together with us."

❧

The Bible is about real life, not dreams. So the people in it are fallible.

❧

The world of the Bible is our world.

❧

There was a Bible reader who found answers to some of his questions but not to others.

"Why isn't everything written in the Bible?" he asked God.
"So that you don't lose the need for the living God,"
God replied.

Someone asked, "Are all of God's words in the Bible?"
"All of God's words cannot be in the Bible," God
answered. "That would mean that God is dead. But
there are enough of God's words in the Bible for people
to know how to live by them."

A disciple asked Jesus, "How should we regard the
Bible? Is it finished?"
Jesus answered, "You should regard the Bible as a God-
given book that lets you make judgments about the
nature of God. The Bible is not finished because not
everything is written in it. The Bible is also finished
because not everything is written in it."

There was a person who really wanted to understand
the Bible, but he was not doing very well.
"Try to understand just two stories," God told him,
"the story of Adam and the story of Jesus. In every
Old Testament story you can see Adam, and every New
Testament story is about Jesus and one of his disciples."

❧

Once upon a time people decided to build a tower reaching to heaven.

They were all of one mind. "We will show God what we can do. We will have the tallest tower in the world."

"I love the people with the smallest tower in the world, too," God said, and he confused their language.

❧

The trouble with the tower of Babel was not that it was too close to God but that it was too far removed from the earth.

❧

Abraham was just an obedient pagan. God chose him because of his obedience, and the Bible began.

❧

God said to Abraham, "Go from your land to a land that I will show you."

"What is better about that land?" Abraham asked.

"It is the land that Adam lost," God said.

"I don't understand," Abraham said nervously.

"When you obey me you gain paradise. When you do not, you lose it," God said to Abraham.

❧

One day God said to Abraham, "Sacrifice your son!" Abraham obeyed. He walked with his son for a long time. The son knew nothing.

"Father, where is the lamb for the sacrifice?" Isaac asked.
"God will provide a lamb for the sacrifice," Abraham replied.
Abraham believed that God was good.

≈

One day God said to Abraham: "You will have to wander
among aliens."
"As you wish," Abraham agreed.
"Other people will not understand the land I want to
give you," God said.

≈

In heaven God said to Abraham, "Everything you did
had profound significance."
"I did not understand any of it," Abraham said.
"But I did," God replied.

≈

In heaven God said to Abraham, "Now you must rest
from all you did on earth."
"I cannot relax here," Abraham said. "I am used to
moving from one place to another."

≈

In heaven God said to Abraham, "Your obedience will be
greatly rewarded here."
"So what is the reward here in heaven?" Abraham asked.
"Understanding what you see," God said.

❧

In heaven God said to Abraham, "You walked the path of Jesus."
"I only went where you told me," Abraham replied.
"My Son did the same," God said to Abraham.

❧

There was a man named Moses. God spoke with him.
"Leave this land," God said. "It is a land of slavery.
Celebrate a festival for me in the wilderness."
Moses obeyed and departed. For forty years he wandered in the wilderness. Then he died.
"Why did you not let me enter the Promised Land?" he asked God.
"You were already in it," God replied.
"How so?" Moses asked.
"Because I was leading you," God said.

❧

The shortest distance between two points is a straight line. By following a straight line one can walk from Egypt to Israel in a few days. Why did it take Moses forty years? Because his was not a path from one point to another, but from one way of thinking to another.

❧

People dislike prophets because prophets are not sent to those who are behaving well.

꙳

There was once a prophet. He told people what God told him.
"The enemy will capture your city," he told them on one
occasion.
"Traitor!" the people cried, and they threw him into a pit.
"I was not the one who thought that up!" he complained
to God. "Let them throw you into the pit instead."
"They threw me into the pit when they put you there,"
God said.

꙳

A prophet is always lonely with God.

꙳

There was a trumpeter whose job was to stand guard
in the tower of the town fortress and warn people if he
saw an enemy approaching. But he happened to live in
peaceful times, and for years he had not had to sound
his trumpet.
One day he could stand it no longer and started
blowing his horn.
The townspeople were terrified. The merchants, clearing
their tables, stored their goods in cellars, others buried
their gold. Still others locked and fortified the city gates
and prepared for battle.
When they realized that no enemy was approaching,
they were furious at the trumpeter and put him to death.
The trumpeter came before God. Feeling guilty he
explained, "I didn't mean to do it. I just had a really
strong urge to blow my trumpet."

"You did right," God comforted him. "Did you not see that the enemy had already taken the whole city? You fell in an unequal fight."

❧

God appeared to Joseph in a dream and said, "Take Mary and the baby and flee from this land to Egypt!" Joseph obeyed. He sensed this was no ordinary dream. "Where are you off to?" his neighbors asked him. "I had a dream," replied Joseph. "He's a strange one," the people said.

❧

Once Mary asked Joseph, "Don't you regret the day we met?" "I never dreamed that all that has happened would happen, but my life would not have been as interesting," Joseph replied.

❧

The apostles were ordinary people because they had to preach their message to all people.

❧

The world was created so that the Bible could be created.
The end of the Bible is the beginning of the end of the world.
The Bible is finished.

❧

The Bible begins with the creation of the world and
ends with the Promised Land. Jesus is the question of
whether the Promised Land is to be found in this world.

❧

God is the way from idolatry to the Promised Land.

❧

The Promised Land is the Garden of Eden again.

❧

God's fairy tales end in reality.

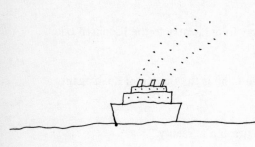

JESUS STANDS ON THE
SHORE AND WATCHES A
SHIP GO BY

A young man stopped at a cafe for a glass of beer. He felt lonely at his little table. Suddenly Jesus walked in. He, too, ordered a beer and sat down at the next table. The two watched each other for a while.

"How should I begin a conversation?" the young man wondered. "It's Jesus, after all."

He raised his glass and acknowledged Jesus. Jesus did the same. But the young man remained the prisoner of his thoughts; and Jesus, slowly finishing his drink, moved to another table.

"An interesting evening," the young man thought; and not seeing Jesus next to him any longer, he felt bolder and began talking about the day's events without worrying about whether Jesus heard him or not.

"An interesting evening," Jesus thought. "I'll have to come back to this cafe."

◈◈◈

Jesus decided to walk the earth again. He climbed down from the crucifix, put on ordinary clothes, and knocked at the door of a certain pastor.

"I am Jesus," he said.

"You can't be," the pastor answered. "Jesus is seated at the right hand of the Father."

"That is true," Jesus continued, "but I have decided to

come and take a look at life on earth."

"But Jesus will come in glory with all his angels," the pastor said emphatically.

"True," Jesus said, "but on that occasion there will be no time to talk with me."

"But I have nothing to say to you," the pastor replied. "I know all about you already."

"That's a pity!" Jesus replied, and he returned to his cross.

◈◈◈◈

One day Jesus decided to take a walk by the sea. He appeared on earth suddenly. No one was ready for him. The day of the Lord came like a thief in the night. Along with some young person Jesus boarded a train, went to the resort town of Lielupe, walked for a while, had a glass of beer with his companion, ate some snacks, and caught the train home.

"A nice Saturday," Jesus said to the youth.

"So it was," the youth replied; and the two of them sat quietly side by side as the Latvian landscape flew by.

◈◈◈◈

It was fall. The leaves had already turned and the mornings were cold.

A flock of crows landed in a field. They talked about various things when suddenly they saw Jesus coming down the road with all his angels.

"What are you doing here?" the crows asked Jesus.

"I just find fall exhilarating," Jesus replied.

೨ல೨ல

Adam asked God, "What do you want to do with me?"
"Turn you into Jesus," God answered.
"Who is Jesus?" Adam asked.
"I am Jesus," God said.
"But I can't become God!" Adam exclaimed.
"I can become you," God explained.

೨ல೨ல

Jesus' words are God's words, minus the abyss between
God and the creation.

೨ல೨ல

In Jesus' words there is no distance between the
creation and the creator, but there is the abyss of God.

೨ல೨ல

When God walked the earth in Jesus, people reproached
Jesus for acting like God.

೨ல೨ல

Jesus was sitting with his disciples.
"Why are you so sad?" the disciples asked.
"I'm lonely," Jesus answered.
"But you're famous," the disciples objected. "Everyone
is talking about you."
"I need a friend," Jesus said. "That old soldier over
there is the only person who understands me."
"But he's a monster, he crucifies people!" the disciples

exclaimed indignantly.

"Yes, but he's not the one who passes judgment on them," Jesus replied.

"We still don't like him," the disciples insisted.

"He is my only friend," Jesus said.

❧❧❧❧

Jesus asked the Father, "Why won't you let me make that old soldier I like so much a disciple?"

"Just let him go on being your friend," the Father replied. "He is a soldier. He has to obey orders. He cannot follow you."

❧❧❧❧

A certain Pharisee was a friend of Jesus. The other Pharisees laughed at him, but he said, "I like this young man Jesus. I understand him."

Jesus liked the lonely Pharisee. A lonely Pharisee and a lonely Jesus. Two friends. Two men who understood each other at once. Two men who understood each other without words. A Pharisee and the Son of God.

❧❧❧❧

Jesus had a friend who was a Pharisee. The Pharisee understood Jesus, but he did not understand the disciples. That was his tragedy. When he was with the disciples he felt like a Pharisee. When he was with the Pharisees he felt like a disciple.

◌◌◌◌

One day Jesus brought a lamb to the Temple. "Sacrifice this for me," he said to the priest.

"For which sins?" the priest asked in a businesslike tone.

"For the sins of all of us," Jesus explained to the priest.

"That is not done," said the priest, and he refused Christ's sacrifice.

◌◌◌◌

In heaven Jesus asked Moses, "What do you think? Why did those who scrupulously fulfilled the Law not accept me?"

Moses replied, "I don't know, and it's a pity. But there seems to be some other path besides yours."

◌◌◌◌

Jesus said to his disciples, "I have not come to reject Moses. I have come to fulfill the Law. I am sorry the Pharisees dislike me."

A disciple said, "Why are you paying attention to them? Look how many people are following you!"

Jesus replied, "The Pharisees try to observe what Moses taught, and my Father spoke with Moses."

◌◌◌◌

Jesus was crucified because his own people hesitated to stone him.

31

୬୬୬୬

The disciples asked Jesus, "What does it mean to say that the day of the Lord will come like a thief in the night? How will you come again?"
"When I come again, no one will recognize me. I will come as one of the least of my flock, and I will judge everyone by how they receive me."

୬୬୬୬

The idea that a human being is God amounts to the issue of whether an image of God can be found in the world. It is not about a miracle-child.

୬୬୬୬

The idea that Jesus is God is popular because the dream "I am God" is to some extent the formula for the world's happiness.

୬୬୬୬

When people accept the notion that Jesus is God, they admit a divine element into the world. The result is saintliness on the one hand and illusions on the other.

୬୬୬୬

When people reject the idea that Jesus is God, they deny the divine element in the world. In the end this means violence and sadness.

◌◌◌◌

To accept the divinity of Jesus is to have faith in the divine element in the world generally.

◌◌◌◌

The truth that the world is not God crucified Jesus. Christianity sprang from the dream that "I am God, if only a little."

◌◌◌◌

Every human being plays God to some extent; so God's Son Jesus will be a problem for human beings as long as humanity exists.

◌◌◌◌

Mary said to Joseph, "My child will rule the world." "He does not look at all like a conqueror," Joseph replied.
Mary said to Joseph, "My son is meek and mild, but when he says something, you think about it for a long time."

◌◌◌◌

Someone asked God, "How should I pray to Jesus?" God replied, "In Jesus you see a human being and God. You should pray to God, but you should treat the human being as a human being."

_ോ◌◌◌_

Mary Magdalene was her parents' only daughter, and
they spoiled her. She was used to doing whatever
she pleased. Gradually she descended into a life of
debauchery. At a certain point Mary realized that evil
powers had taken command of her and that she was no
longer able to oppose them. She was frightened, but she
did not know what to do. Then, by chance, she heard
about Jesus.

At first Jesus scolded her saying, "I cannot help people
who will not help themselves."

Mary replied, "I do not have the strength to help
myself."

Jesus said to her, "I have been sent to those who know
they are sinners."

"I do not know what it means not to be a sinner," Mary
replied.

Jesus told her, "If you know that, you will be with me in
paradise."

And he ordered the demons to leave Mary, and from
that moment on she followed Jesus.

_ോ◌◌◌_

A girl fell in love with Jesus. Her name was Mary
Magdalene. Jesus had cast out her demons. She idolized
Jesus. Jesus did not quite understand her. Jesus was
holy. Mary was an ordinary sinner. They were together
for a long time and developed feelings for each other.
Mary saw that Jesus was headed for the cross. He did

not abandon Mary. Mary did not abandon him.
"Do not abandon that girl," God had told Jesus. "You should not abandon a girl who loves you."

~~~

Mary Magdalene asked Jesus, "Why do you dislike it when people worship you?"
Jesus replied, "I am a man. I like it better when people make friends with me. Still, my Father has said that I am incarnate love, and love is worthy of worship. God is love."

~~~

Jesus said to Mary Magdalene, "You are a great sinner, but I love you."
Mary Magdalene replied, "You are holy, but I love you, too."

~~~

"Where are you from?" some people asked Jesus.
"From the heavens," Jesus replied.
"Do not blaspheme!" they exclaimed. "We know you are from Nazareth."
"There are heavens in Nazareth, too," Jesus replied.

~~~

Jesus asked Judas, "Do you love me?"
"Everyone loves you," Judas replied.
Jesus asked again, "Do you love me?"

"People have to love you, you are the Son of God,"
Judas replied.

Jesus said, "Why don't you love me, Judas?"

Judas became alarmed and said, "I do love you."

Jesus sighed. "I love you, Judas," he said. "I feel that
something very painful is going to happen between us."

✤✤✤✤

Jesus said to the Father, "I am lonely. I need some
friends."

"Choose twelve disciples for yourself," God proposed to
Jesus.

"Will they be my friends?" Jesus asked the Father.

"Yes, but one of them will betray you."

"Then why should he be my disciple?"

"So that all your disciples can identify with him when
each of them from time to time doubts your words,"
God replied to Jesus.

✤✤✤✤

The apostle John said to Judas, "What are you thinking
about all the time?"

Judas replied, "I am thinking about what our teacher says."

"You shouldn't think about it so much. You should just
believe it," John said.

"I want to understand what I believe," Judas replied.

"We are human beings, he is the Son of God," John
said. "To understand him is to understand God."

"I still want to understand him," Judas said.

"We can only worship him," John replied.

"It is not right to worship a human being," Judas said.

"He is more than a human being," John said.

"So it seems to me, too, sometimes," Judas said. "I see him as a prophet."

"I don't know what he is, but he speaks like God," John said. "I just love him."

"I admire him, too," Judas said, "but I am afraid he will dismantle everything that Moses built."

"He does not reject Moses," John said.

"He places himself above Moses," Judas replied.

"The Father has given him power. Look at what is happening—the sick are cured, miracles are occurring. If God did not support him, all this could not happen."

"I believe he has been sent by God," Judas said, "but he adds something of his own as well."

"He is the Son of God, he can do that," John replied.

⁄øøøʊ

Judas asked Jesus, "Why did you choose me?"

Jesus answered, "My Father told me that I had to have a disciple who did not agree with me about everything. My Father pointed you out to me."

⁄øøøʊ

In heaven the apostle Paul said to Jesus, "I thought about you a great deal, but I never would have come to know you if you had not struck me blind on the road to Damascus."

Jesus replied to Paul, "The blindest person of all is the one who thinks he understands me as God. One can understand me only as a human being. You have experienced me as God. Let us now get to know each other as human beings."

* əəəə*

Jesus' law is the law of love and freedom.

əəəə

If you know Jesus it is impossible not to love him. Those who do not love Jesus do not know him.

əəəə

Obedience is one path to God, freedom is another. In Jesus the two paths come together.

əəəə

Once when he was still a child Jesus asked his Father, "Why do I never laugh?"
"That comes from me," God replied. "I love everything and never make fun of anything."

əəəə

Jesus raised Lazarus from the dead, but Lazarus did not understand why. He liked being dead.
"I can give you a second life," Jesus said to Lazarus.
"One life was already too much," Lazarus answered.
"I know I can give you something more," Jesus replied.

"What?" Lazarus asked.

"The secret of eternal life," Jesus answered.

"And what is that?"

"Me," Jesus said.

◦◦◦◦◦

Jesus raised Lazarus from the dead.

"It's morning," Jesus said to Lazarus.

"So I'm alive again," Lazarus said, unpleasantly surprised. "It is not as beautiful here as it is on the other side."

Jesus wept. He loved Lazarus. He wanted Lazarus to live.

"There is life after death," Lazarus said.

Jesus fell silent.

"Do not be alarmed," the Father said to Jesus. "For the time being you must not see that beauty."

◦◦◦◦◦

Jesus was drinking wine with a centurion.

"It's a tough business being a soldier," Jesus said.

"So it is," the centurion replied, "but my men love me."

"Why?" Jesus asked.

"I really don't know," the centurion confessed.

◦◦◦◦◦

Jesus said to the Father, "I don't want to be crucified. I want all people to love me."

"That's not possible," God replied. "Not all people do

the will of God. Those who do not do the will of God are never going to like you."

∽✸✸✸✒

Jesus asked the Father, "Why do people want to stone me?"

"They do not understand you," God said, "and it is just as well they don't."

"Why?" Jesus asked.

"Because your job is to show them what God is like. You are not an ordinary person."

∽✸✸✸✒

Jesus asked his Father, "Why do you want to condemn me to death?"

"Because for the time being your teachings are too lofty for human beings," God replied.

∽✸✸✸✒

"What is purgatory?" a youth once asked Jesus.

"The bushes where Adam hid from God," Jesus replied.

"And what does that mean?"

"It means there is a place where you can avoid looking God in the eye."

❦❦❦

Accepting Jesus into your life is a single act, but becoming like Jesus is a long process of living with the living Jesus, living in the living Jesus, and letting Jesus live in your life.

❦❦❦

The presence of the living Jesus in your life does not contradict the Holy Scriptures; it helps you understand them better.

❦❦❦

Living in Jesus means living in the world of the Bible. The world of the Bible is a world of souls.

❦❦❦

God cannot draw closer to creation than God did in Jesus.

❦❦❦

Jesus lived.
"I will have nothing more to say about myself," God said.

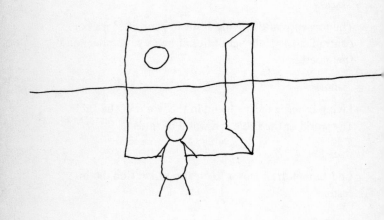

IN FRONT OF ME
THERE IS A LITTLE
WINDOW ON A BIG
WORLD

4
Thinking

There was a philosopher who had written many books and considered himself wise. He had something to say about God, the world, and lots of other subjects.

One morning he was shaving. Before him in the mirror he saw a man with a lathered face and tired eyes.

"Hi, friend!" the philosopher said. Suddenly he began thinking, "What is this I am looking at?"

All his earlier conceptions collapsed, and he grew deeply perplexed. Often he stood before the mirror thinking, "Is this image real or not?"

He found no answer to his question, grew old, died, and came before God.

"What was I missing?" he asked God. "Why couldn't I answer such a simple question?"

"It was not a simple question," God replied. "While you were looking in the mirror, you understood more than you did in the rest of your life put together."

∿

There was a philosopher named Socrates. He fancied he knew something. He fancied he knew that he knew nothing.

"You are just a little too fancy," Jesus told him in heaven.

~

A child looked at the sea.
"I want to be like you," the child said.
"You can't do much more than play with the stones on the shore," the sea said.
"I am so little," the child said sadly.
"Happiness is the art of being little," the sea replied.

~

Human beings are a mystery to themselves.

~

Nothing I understand explains me.

~

Everything begins with the thought "I am" and ends with the thought "I am." In between are dreams of wisdom.

~

First of all the world thinks, "I just am." Then, "How should I live?" Then once again, "I just am."

~

Human beings are more than they understand.

~

Real events are mental events. The world is a theater of ideas.

~

An idea is a fruit of the Spirit, not a material product.

~

A human being is an animal with an idea.

~

Ideas govern, matter serves.

~

The mire creates the desire to fly.

~

In the world there are ideas and pastries. Pastries prevail in this world, ideas in the next.

~

There was a little girl who collected candy. She did everything imaginable to obtain it. But when she got a new piece of candy, she did not eat it but put it in a special drawer in her desk.

"Why do you just collect candy but not eat it?" God asked her.

"Because when you put it in your mouth it doesn't last long," the girl replied.

"You have understood more about heaven than many a professor," God said.

45

～

Love of ideas is a kind of asceticism; eroticism flourishes where there are no ideas.

～

An idea is the opposite of eating and sex. Only ideas go to heaven.

～

When eroticism and ideas intersect they make a world worth living in.

～

The world has a dream. The dream is never evil.

～

The world dreams of not being itself.

～

The world wants you to focus on its dreams, not its nakedness.

～

Dreams help us not to focus on the mire.

～

Dreams are moments when we forget we are not God.

~

We long for spirit, not objects.

~

Only spirit, not objects, can be investigated forever.

~

Truth is usually neutral; the person who knows it is not.

~

The world finds happiness not by knowing itself but by looking for something in itself that is divine.

~

Self-knowledge brings happiness only to God.

~

To know the truth about yourself you need to know the truth about God.

~

You can think about God by examining yourself.

~

You can think forever about something only if it is linked to God.

~

The questions a soul lives with should be greater, not smaller, than itself.

～

You cannot understand a truth that is larger than yourself.

～

"To be or not to be?"—that is a deep question. "How should I live?"—that is a small and gratifying question.

～

The question "How should I live?" always reverts to the question "To be or not to be?" because the world cannot be as God is.

～

It is not peace that the world needs as much as something it finds interesting.

～

The thought "I just am" makes us happy; "I am beautiful" is a detail.

～

The thought "I just am" leads to God. The thought "What am I really doing?" makes us aware of our utter insignificance.

～

The last great thought is "Everything is." After that come our favorite trivialities.

~

Human beings are either animals or theologians.

~

The world's boundaries are the soul's boundaries.

~

Every soul is a little center of the world.

~

The real moment is always this moment, the real place is always here.

~

There was a clock on the table in a pub.
"What time is it?" God asked.
"Life," the clock replied.

~

Every day is a mini-lifetime.

~

Time walks. Fools run.

~

Speed slows down the race of life.

~

To be ahead of time is to be late.

~

If you know life from A to Z, there is no point in living it.

~

Ideas do not arise from contemplating emptiness but from contemplating God or the world.

~

Emptiness is an invitation to think.

~

In the world there are only two way of achieving anything: praying for God's help and knowing how the world is put together.

~

You can meditate on God and eternity or on the moment and emptiness. These are the two ends of the line.

~

In a soul there is either an icon or emptiness.

~

Do not let small truths give you the illusion that you are great.

~

Every person understands God in some small measure. Being satisfied with that small measure is idolatry.

~

Everyone who understands God is mistaken.

~

Absolute truths are not meant for human beings
because we are not absolute beings.

~

God does not scold us for having imperfect ideas about
God.

~

Do not let the vain attempt to understand
transcendence lead you away from God altogether.

~

In the face of ultimate truth you should be quiet. In the
face of your own foolishness you can sermonize.

~

Contemplating something exalted does not produce
happiness because you recognize that you are not
exalted. Contemplating something ugly so that you
seem beautiful by comparison is pathetic.

~

Whether human beings can be eternal or not depends
on their capacity to think about the idea "God exists."

~

The world does not let you reduce it to a theory; the only truth that pleases the world is "The world just is."

~

Either the world thinks about being or it just goes around in circles.

~

Either the world is an object of spiritual meditation or it becomes very tiresome.

~

A temporary world cannot understand being.

~

The world can understand symbols, but not real life.

~

Truth governs on the sly, hiding behind myth.

~

In the world there will always be two truths existing side by side.

~

Truth does not win arguments because there are at least two truths.

~

It is risky for the world to understand the truth about itself.

~

At bedtime, telling stories is more advisable than telling the truth.

~

Truths were not born with the world. They are all part of God.

~

It is God's existence in the world that makes logic possible; logic comes from God, not from material nature.

~

Logic is an angel's sword.

~

Truth is as old as God; our ideas about it are modern.

~

An idea can be a new discovery, but not a novelty.

~

You have to wander to seek truth.

~

Ideas do not come to a person who already feels wise.

53

∾

Happy people do not philosophize.

∾

Wisdom is a good thing provided you have neither too much nor too little of it.

∾

On the path to truth you come up against the truth which you yourself are.

∾

Focus your thinking on God, not the world, because a wise nullity is tragic.

∾

A nullity is great when it suffers, not when it is enjoying itself.

∾

The world should not make peace with its own insignificance.

∾

There was an artist who loved to draw. One day he drew a zero.
"That, too, is something interesting," God said.

∾

When an idea becomes tolerant it becomes creative.

~

Ideas need room when they emerge from a monk's cell.

~

Tolerance created the world. Purity of dogma abolishes the world.

~

The world is not a dogma but a dialogue of dogmas.

~

Our dogmas put a face on the world.

~

The world is found somewhere between dogmas on the one hand and atheism on the other.

~

A single truth is an error.

~

A conclusion is a transition from one conviction to another.

~

The world is the diversity of a single principle.

~

The world rests upon the concord, not the conflict, of opposites.

～

The world is the unity of opposites that goes by the name of everyday life.

～

The person who thinks the world constantly repeats itself understands it.

～

The thought that "this is just the way the world is" brings sadness. The thought that "the world just is" brings happiness.

～

You can take pleasure in the idea "I am," and you can take pleasure in the idea "There is something else as well."

～

The world's happiness lies in the dream that it is in some small measure God.

～

The world feels like a weekday.

～

The world is mysterious; it treats everybody differently.

～

The world does not love the truth about itself.

~

The world likes being led.

~

Only for the person who wants to be God does God not exist.

~

We can remember the beginning of the world; we cannot remember the beginning of God.

~

God is a mystery which you can contemplate only through yourself.

~

Thinking about God demands asceticism because it focuses on something other than yourself. If you just want to be what you are, you need eroticism.

~

Only in solitude do you come to understand God because you are God's one-and-only.

~

There are ideas that arise from the fact that "I exist" and ideas that arise from the fact that "God exists." The two need to come together for life to be meaningful.

~

You can think "I am like God" or "God is like me"; otherwise you cannot think about God at all.

~

Wisdom greater than your own will always seem a bit foolish to you.

~

A creature needs to know there is always something it does not know.

~

An angel thought, "Infinity always looks unfinished."

~ .

The world needs to feel a little immoral to keep from playing the role of a second God.

~

If you think about God theoretically, you will only invent a new idol.

~

The reality of God is something about which differences of opinion are all of one mind.

~

A God beyond images allows us to dream.

58

~

God's Spirit is not symmetrical.

~

People may dare to be wise if they have a sense of humor because wisdom ends in paradox.

~

Ideas are only as deep as the thinker's view of God.

~

You can understand life on earth only by keeping heaven in mind.

~

Reality conceals itself from the person who believes there is no God.

~

Human beings are made for God.

~

Someone drew a circle on the beach.
"I know the secret of infinity," the circle said.
A wave splashed on the beach and carried off part of the circle. "Infinity is alive," said the sea.

~

Reverence for reality spells the end of atheism.

THE SEA DWELLS
QUIETLY BESIDE ME

5

God and the World

One day the sun was shining, the snow was melting, and a breath of spring was in the air. God decided to take a walk. He came down from heaven and in a relaxed mood made a loop through a suburban neighborhood.

"Why are you doing this?" the angels asked.

"I just like it around here," God replied.

A city was going about its business one winter. Conductors were taking tickets on the trams. The passengers were thinking their thoughts. The river that flowed through the city slept peacefully under the ice. Monuments commemorated bygone eras. Fresh snow had fallen.

"What an insubstantial beauty!" thought the monuments, gazing at the snow.

"What a meaningless attempt to stop the flow of time!" thought the snow, contemplating the monuments.

The world rests on the dogma, God exists; there is no other dogma.

God is who God is, and there is nothing to be done about it.

God created the world.
"That is your most mysterious work," the angels said.
"And also my favorite," God replied.

In Eden an angel said, "The world is a mystery. It is not God, and it is not the opposite of God."

In everything there is something of God to discuss.

You can find God anywhere provided you do not call the world God.

The world does not explain itself.

Do not venture to explore the world's depths if you have no appreciation for God's tolerance.

The world is the mask, not the face, of God.

One angel said to another: "The world is a mask God hides behind."
"He puts it on so that no one will fear infinity," the other angel agreed.

God is human because God created human beings in the image of God.

Human beings are God's favorite problem.

Adam asked God, "Why do you let yourself be disobeyed?"
"So that creation will understand that God is free," God replied.

Freedom and the will of God make for a beautiful world, not one without the other.

An angel asked God, "Why are there so many human beings?"
"Because each person is called to learn about one aspect of God," God replied.

❧

God loves simple people because, often enough, it is only the simple who see God as God.

❧

The simple know enough to love God. God will always be a riddle to the wise.

❧

There was a time when God lacked you. So he made the world.

❧

The world is not an enjoyable place when only its own desires are realized.

❧

In Adam's world there needs to be more than just Adam's ideas.

❧

Perfection is the world plus God.

❧

The world is made for the moment; the soul is made for eternity.

❧

The world is a unity in diversity, not a dogma.

God's mind is so vast that it hides itself from the world so as not to terrify the creation.

The world is the answer to the quarrel between dogmas and emptiness.

When approaching the world God puts on a mask, for God is wholly other than the world.

God is not-world. Hence the world's dreams are necessarily theological.

God shields the world from the truth about itself by giving it dreams.

Only God, not the world, understands the world.

The world is the child, not the mirror, of God.

God had an idea, namely the world. Interest in the idea continues.

In creating the world God willed to create an icon.

God creates the world, the world creates dreams.

The world does not love its own nature but the hand of God that shaped it.

The world should not try to think about God apart from the world.

God is transcendent; so is the world's true nature.

The world needs to stand at a certain distance from God, neither too near, nor too far away.

The world loves perfection that does not destroy it.

The world is dear to God as it is.

The wisdom of God is the beauty of the world.

Everything is beautiful when you find traces of God in it.

Some idea of God's is to be found in every particle of the world.

Nature is living theology.

There is a lot of God, which is why there have to be trillions of leaves on the trees and trillions of grains of sand on the shore.

There are no things that can reflect God and no things that do not reflect God.

The world revolves around God. God takes walks in the world.

There is no creature that can understand God completely. There is no creature that cannot understand something of God.

In Eden an angel said, "The world does not seem to be as God planned it, but all the same, God's plan will come to pass."

"Explain that!" the other angels asked.

"Creation's ideas are different from the creator's, but the creator will reach an understanding with creation."

In Eden an angel said, "God has a plan for the world but does not hold to it too strictly."

"Explain that!" the other angels asked.

"God departs from the plan whenever something worthy of God's attention comes about in the world process."

God does not govern the world too strictly. God wants to see the world living its own life.

God's plans leave room for creation's dreams.

God leaves some of the world's dreams unrealized so that there is room for God's dreams, too.

"What will the end of the world be like?" a young person asked God.

"The two of us will think it up together, that's how it will be," God said to the youth.
"I don't understand," the youth said.
"I am looking at you right now and thinking," God said.

Governing the world is a hard job—the whole world watches you.

Governing the world means loving the worst creature in the world.

In Eden an angel said, "The world can never be finished."
"Explain that!" the other angels asked.
"God is infinite," the angel said, "and so are God's wishes for the world."

Adam asked God, "When will you consider your work finished?"
"When it has become completely simple in every respect," God replied.
"Why so?" Adam asked.
"Because I am not complicated," God replied. "For example, I am simply love."

In Eden an angel said, "God has many faces."
"Explain that!" the other angels asked.
"Each of God's creatures is a face of God."

In Eden an angel said, "God is a mystery that reveals itself only gradually."
"Explain that!" the other angels said.
"Creation has limits and can make God out only gradually."

In Eden an angel said, "The world is always running away from God, then regretting it."
"Explain that!" the other angels asked.
"The world fears being small," the angel said, "yet without God it has no significance."

The world likes to dream that God exists; it does not like to think that there is no God.

The world flirts more than it quarrels with God.

The world often forgets God. God does not forget the world.

God created the world to live a common life with it.

The world was created to delight in God, not in itself.

The world can admire God, but imitating God is difficult.

Even when it imitates God, a creature remains a creature.

A creature's difference from God is the source of both its happiness and its suffering.

In Eden an angel said, "The world does not seem to know why it exists, for unlike God it makes all sorts of demands."

The struggle for perfection prompts impatience with God for creating the world.

The world knows perfection only when it seeks God.

The world is wonderful and terrible at the same time.
The world is terrible so that you can understand God,
who is not terrible.

The world is not meant to be worshipped.

When a creature's thoughts and God's thoughts differ,
the creature thinks God does not love it.

A creature thinks God was right to create it, but wrong
to create some other creature that does not love it.

When God has a new idea, it changes the world.

God is great. God's dreams are, too.

God's power is peaceful and quiet. God does not
advertise it. People usually do not notice it.

Someone was walking by the sea and said, "You are
infinite, just like God."
"I have a horizon," the sea replied.

God's nature is God's only limitation.

Four angels were having a discussion:
"God has departed from the earth, for otherwise God
would have to destroy the disobedient."
"God would rather retreat than destroy."
"The earth will think it has defeated God."
"Victory over God is its punishment."

God wants you to seek God. Begin with the prayer,
"Help me, God, to find you in the world." Saying it once
is enough.

The God we seek out there we usually find right here.

The world exists.
God exists, too.
The world exists.
Seek God in it.

THERE IS NO WAY
BACK TO THE BEAUTIFUL
PLACE WHERE I ONCE WAS

6

Religion

In the beginning religion is fact, then fact plus myth. This is the golden age of religion. Eventually religion becomes nothing but myth, and people stop thinking about what it means. At that point God creates a new fact.

≈

The world is unhappy if nothing but facts exist because the world by itself is not the truth.

≈

The world prefers myths to facts because the world is the fruit of God's imagination.

≈

There is the truth that God exists, and there is the mythology based on this affirmation.

≈

The world covers its nakedness with myths.

≈

The world does not like to see its evil. It covers itself with myths.

≈

God tells us stories rather than the truth to protect us from the reality that we are not God.

≈

The fantasy that I am divine creates myths. The reality that I am not God creates the need for consolation.

≈

A myth lives when there is a measure of truth in it.

≈

Encountering the transcendence of truth, people want a myth.

≈

Idols arise because of the transcendence of God.

≈

Even an idol signifies "God exists."

≈

Idolatry arises from the desire to see God.

≈

Idolatry is bondage to our own fantasies.

≈

An idol is an attempt to invent a better God than God.

People make good idols when they believe that a tree is actually God.

Absolute truths become idols because they are unattainable.

Idols displease God, but God puts up with them.

You cannot avoid idols, but you can refuse to kiss them.

Idols oppose atheism; God opposes idols.

Idols need a sacrificial victim; God opposes them by giving gifts.

If someone fears being honest to God, he is thinking of an idol, not God.

God wants you to look him in the eye. An idol does not.

Before a petty idol, piety looks grand.

The wealth with which an idol is surrounded is poverty for the spirit.

Religion perishes when it is nothing but correct conduct before an idol.

A prophet is the only way out of idolatry.

Religion begins with an unrecognized prophet and ends with an orthodox attitude toward an idol of the prophet.

God's personality disturbs the world. Only idols are gratifying.

We begin with idols, we end with the question, "Who is Jesus?"

You cannot think forever about idols; about God you can.

Dogma is necessary to begin with. For paradise you need your own ideas about God.

The only dogma that is absolutely necessary is "God exists." The rest will not survive eternity.

Dogmas arise from truth and the finitude of the world.

We are separated from the highest truths by a door on which dogmas are inscribed.

Dogmas are an attempt to understand a dream.

Dogmas are a representation of God, not God.

The church is the result of dogma. Dogmas need incense.

God leaves stories behind, churches leave dogmas behind.

Prophets leave parables behind, dogmas leave idols.

Life is the opposite of dogma.

Purity of dogma rules out the possibility of a world.

Real life is a little heretical; only within the walls of the church can dogmas be perfectly observed.

Dogmas safeguard spirituality in the world as long as we think about them rather than worship them.

Sound dogmas deny themselves for the sake of peace.

Dogmas need a rest now and then.

Religion always needs a little reformation.

Only a heretic has searched seriously for God.

Heresy results from God's infinity.

A heretic is not happy. An idol worshipper is happy.

A religion is alive when it has a lot of unburned heretics.

There was a grand inquisitor who did his work with
zeal, making sure that all people thought correctly.
As for those who did not, he tortured them until they
changed their mind. He died with the feeling of a job
well done and came before God.
"I have decided to give you a taste of what you did to
others," God said to him.
The inquisitor did not understand. "How can this be?
Everything I did, I did for your glory."
"I would have preferred it if my glory had suffered a
little damage," God replied.
"But I always believed that repentant heretics would go
to heaven," the inquisitor said.
"So they will," God replied. "And so will you when you
have experienced what they did."

There was an ardent Catholic who spent all his wealth
on the struggle against Protestantism. He died and went
to paradise. Jesus asked him, "What reward do you want
for all you have done?"
The Catholic replied, "I don't know which one to choose."

Jesus said to him, "Then take a little walk in the paradise of the Protestants, and afterwards we will talk about this some more."

❧

Sound dogmas make saints. Wanting everyone to be a saint makes inquisitors.

❧

An inquisitor is born of the idea, "I know all there is to know about God."

❧

The word "God" is rarely used by people who understand God.

❧

The true God rarely goes by the name "God."

❧

The idea of God is an idol; God's spirit is not.

❧

Theology is for atheists. The world is usually content with the fact that God exists.

❧

Theology is talking about God when God is not in the room.

Theology is a riddle which God invented for heaven.

The world should not be condemned for not recognizing God, for icons are not God.

Only a man-made image of God frightens people; the real God does not.

If you think God tries to frighten people as Satan does, you do not know God.

The world loves dressing up a bit and playing God.

Piety performs rituals because the world as it naturally behaves is not good.

The world makes crèches to make amends for the real Bethlehem.

The world devises pretty crucifixes so that Christianity can base itself on something beautiful, not on something monstrous where you see the evil of the world.

You can swap money for God by buying a small crucifix.
God is amused by how little God costs.

Pretty crucifixes do not save.

Pretty crucifixes are the end of Christianity.

Religion states its case with icons. Atheism replies with
irony.

An icon is a memorial of God. It should not be God's
memorial stone.

An icon does not depict God but what a soul finds
sacred.

You do not get tired of icons if you sense the will of
God in them.

At a party the cake should not be the center of attention.

There was a great enemy of icons. He regarded icons as idols and was an active iconoclast. One day he died. He came before God, and God asked him: "Why did you so despise the images of my Son?"

"I thought it was forbidden to fashion an image of God," the man answered.

"So it is," God said, "but that is exactly what my Son had to do."

There was an icon painter who was very religious and showed the greatest respect for images of Jesus. One day he saw Jesus in a dream.

"You know me only by my face," Jesus said. "I want you to get to know me better."

"How should I do that?" the painter asked.

"Try to understand that I am everywhere."

"I don't understand," the painter said.

"My image leads to my Father," Jesus said, "and there is no place where God is not."

God's will leaves living icons of itself in the world.

Children are the real icons.

Fasting arises from the attempt to combine God with feasting.

When Christianity focuses exclusively on death on the cross, it becomes intolerant and aggressive.

Christianity should be more than kissing the crucifix.

God does not want sacrificial deaths but peaceful lives.

The older a religion, the more dreams it acquires. When it becomes nothing but dreams, there is an awakening.

The truest religion is an old one with a little heresy of our own mixed in.

Saints are authorized idols.

Saints are necessary so that you do not end up praying to icons that are nothing but wood.

Saints are Christianity's answer to the Pharisees of Judaism.

Stories of the saints' spiritual journeys, not their shrines, are efficacious.

A person who reveres God usually reveres the pastor as well. A pastor has a difficult job because people view him almost as God.

A certain pastor could not seem to behave properly. He was always saying the wrong thing or doing something that pastors should not do. He was very unhappy and asked God to help him start living a proper life.

"God, can you teach me to live a proper life?" the pastor asked.

"Of course, I can" God replied. "But first you have to decide what you want to be—a pastor or a proper person."

"Can't I be both at the same time?" the pastor asked in surprise.

"No," God answered with a sigh, "because I am already short of people who understand others."

There was a man who had sinned much in his life but then became a pastor. His ways had not really changed

much, and the other pastors did not particularly like him.
One day Jesus came to see him. "Hi, friend!" Jesus said.
"Aren't you Jesus?" the pastor asked.
"I'm glad at least one pastor recognizes me," Jesus
replied.

≈

A cloud once said to a church, "How can you tell people
about heaven? After all, you reside on earth."
The church answered him, "Human beings do not
understand what you tell them. They, too, live on earth."

≈

You cannot live in God's house but you can visit it as a
guest. Every guest receives a favor.

≈

Jesus was born on a certain day. Over time, people began
celebrating it as a holiday, and the period leading up to it
became a great shopping season. Shopkeepers decorated
their windows and offered bargains, and people bought as
much as their resources allowed.
"Father, it seems to me that something is wrong here," Jesus
said to God one day. "I was poor and preached a kingdom
not of this world. And my realm is available for free."
"There's nothing to be done about it," God replied.
"People celebrate as they see fit. It is better for them
to buy things while remembering your birthday than to
forget about it altogether."

There was once a young man who took a liking to a certain cross. It was very large, heavy, and beautiful. He put the cross on his wall.

"That is not your cross," God told him. "But leave it on the wall for the time being. We will bear it together."

Jesus said to his Father: "I don't like decorations in churches."

"They have to be there," God explained. "They are a healthy illusion."

"I don't understand," Jesus said.

"People need to have some idea of paradise," the Father said to Jesus.

"Well, it is certainly very beautiful here in heaven. But for the time being we should not let this be known, since suicide will not get a person here!" Jesus replied.

"Right," the Father of Jesus agreed. "That is the sort of thing a child might dream up."

"But childhood is a holy thing," Jesus said.

"So it is," the Father of Jesus replied.

TWO PEOPLE EYE
EACH OTHER CAUTIOUSLY.
ANGELS NUDGE THEM
CLOSER TOGETHER.

7

Ethics and Politics

There was once a secret agent, so secret that only God knew about him.

"Tell me what is happening in Latvia," God said to him.

"Nothing is happening there," the agent replied.

"That's suspicious," God said. "Something is happening everywhere, but nothing is happening in Latvia? I should go and take a look around."

∽⌾⌾⌾

There was a newly independent country. Many things were not in good shape there. People were dissatisfied most of the time.

"What a country this is!" they said to each other.

"People steal and worry only about themselves."

"The country is as you have made it," God told them.

"But we have a proposal."

"What sort of proposal?" the people asked.

"What about letting us govern your state?" God proposed.

"But that means we'll have to go to church every day," the people replied, "we won't be able to enjoy ourselves, and the clergy will meddle with things they don't understand."

"We see the matter quite differently," God replied. "All you have to do is let us be part of whatever it is that you are doing."

✒✒✒

God and Satan were discussing Lenin. Satan said, "See how holy Lenin is. He loves the poor, he does not commit adultery; and all this I have accomplished without your help."
"But he will go to hell when he dies," God observed.
"I just wanted to show you that a person can be holy without God," Satan replied.
"But that person will be terribly unhappy," God said.
"That is no concern of mine," Satan replied. "I did not want you to create human beings in the first place. See how quickly they deny you as soon as someone puts them up to it. Just recognize your mistake and leave everything as it was before Adam existed."

✒✒✒

Freedom is the discovery that you exist.

✒✒✒

A free person needs God more than an unfree person because a free person has more choices to make.

✒✒✒

Free emotions are beautiful but hard to manage.

∞∞∞∞

Freedom often stimulates bad behavior because the world is not a second God.

∞∞∞∞

Freedom strips us naked.

∞∞∞∞

To serve God is the only way to preserve freedom.
A person who serves God is free forever.
A person who does not serve God serves Satan.

∞∞∞∞

Every person has a particular way of serving God.
The most beautiful kind of service is the one God gives you.

∞∞∞∞

Each person has a special place in God's plans.
Human freedom is also in God's plans.

∞∞∞∞

The world has a right to its desires, but its desires must not be fulfilled, for in that case it would know too much about itself.

∞∞∞∞

When you fulfill your fantasies you come to know yourself, which is something only God can feel good about.

❧❧❧❧

The world does not like those who know it too well.

❧❧❧❧

The world does not like being known. God does.

❧❧❧❧

The world wants people to dress it up, not undress it.

❧❧❧❧

The world likes a low-cut evening dress, but not actual nakedness.

❧❧❧❧

The world is honest, but only with God. For everyone else it has devised good manners.

❧❧❧❧

Only God is permitted to be totally honest in polite society.

❧❧❧❧

Without a code of conduct the world is forced to see its own ugliness.

❧❧❧❧

Ethics cannot be rejected altogether because the world is not happy with itself as it is.

A person who thinks he is evil dreams of goodness. A person who thinks he is good tells everybody else they are evil.

A lofty idea reproaches you to some extent; a base idea says, "You are great."

It is the person who does not want to do evil, not the person who wants to be good, who does good.

The desire for perfection is cruel, not virtuous.

People who know there is something wrong with them seek God's commandments. People who think they are good teach God how to live.

The world depends on those who are not especially convinced that the world depends on them.

The world depends on the sinner's desire to reform, not on the saints.

✷✷✷✷

The prodigal son did not love his village; his brother did. But it was the prodigal who became a celebrity in the village while the righteous brother was only his brother.

✷✷✷✷

It is not the conquest of evil but its non-destruction that brings peace.

✷✷✷✷

The world should not make a habit of observing its own wickedness; it does better to watch stupid but good-natured old Hollywood films.

✷✷✷✷

Happiness does not depend on some great accomplishment but on tolerance of your own insignificance.

✷✷✷✷

Happiness has small measurements.

✷✷✷✷

No one who focuses on himself is happy, for the world is wicked. Happy is the person who focuses on God, who is no fault-finder.

◦◦◦◦

We are often honest only behind each other's backs because we do not understand tolerance.

◦◦◦◦

In the world you can choose to be lonely or to be tolerant.

◦◦◦◦

Striving for perfection leads to intolerance.

◦◦◦◦

Tolerance is the tie that binds truths together; it is a third truth between black and white.

◦◦◦◦

Strict principles collide with truth.

◦◦◦◦

A love of diversity steers the world.

◦◦◦◦

God creates diversity so that everyone has something to talk about with everyone else.

◦◦◦◦

Whatever bears good fruit should be revered. God is secure enough to let anyone dream there is a God.

ഇഇഇ

The world presumes to know its needs better than God does. Thus politics arises.

ഇഇഇ

When a place is a mess, someone who thinks he is better than God has been at work there.

ഇഇഇ

People seek truth in times of change. In a stable regime hierarchy is truth.

ഇഇഇ

Times of change never please those who brought them about.

ഇഇഇ

The majority will always prevail and will always be unhappy with its victory.

ഇഇഇ

Being a leader is not happiness; the more powerful the leader, the less he dares to dream.

ഇഇഇ

Power makes you busy, not happy.

ഇഇഇ

Power makes no one happy except God.

≈≈≈

Wrongdoers need power, honest people can just live.

≈≈≈

In Eden an angel said, "Governing is the art of being last."
"Explain that!" the others asked.
"The state exists for the common man," the angel said.

≈≈≈

People ought to recognize themselves in their president.

≈≈≈

Order in the state comes from order in the soul. Honest
politics creates spiritual power.

≈≈≈

When power lacks even a modicum of spirituality, tanks
will not help.

≈≈≈

Cunning carried to an extreme turns into stupidity.

≈≈≈

Evil is pragmatic; God is not.

≈≈≈

Honest politics results in lasting friends; dishonest
politics gives you a moment of evil power.

◦◦◦◦

Everyone cannot be friends with each other, but it is possible to have no enemies.

◦◦◦◦

Heaping honors on people diminishes our love for them.

◦◦◦◦

The destiny of a few individuals is to become myths. They are rarely happy people.

◦◦◦◦

Love of fame is the desire to get from the world what only God can give.

◦◦◦◦

To be famous is to be naked.

◦◦◦◦

Politics is the art of knowing people, not running things.

◦◦◦◦

Politics is about human relations. Human relations should lead to heaven, not hell.

◦◦◦◦

A king is a public person. Either he embodies his subjects' dreams or a revolution dethrones him. But those who cut off a king's head become slaves, not kings.

✦✦✦✦

The kings who lose power are those who think they are the real rulers.

✦✦✦✦

An aristocrat is someone the servants have made.

✦✦✦✦

Not everyone can be a king. Everyone can be servants.

✦✦✦✦

The true ruler is the one who knows that God rules.

✦✦✦✦

The world likes being governed. It does not like governing itself.

✦✦✦✦

The greater the power, the greater the need for high moral standards.

✦✦✦✦

When people refuse to support a prophet they get to support a conqueror.

✦✦✦✦

A country that does not treasure a prophet is punished by being made to see its own mundane nature.

◦❀❀❀

The world needs a prophet to keep it from theorizing that it is a little like God.

◦❀❀❀

Latvia has a prophet's budget—that is to say, a small one.

◦❀❀❀

Nowadays a prophet has to be a millionaire to be believed.

◦❀❀❀

Either politics is about ideas or it is nothing but intrigue.

◦❀❀❀

A weak state is the result of a bankrupt idea.

◦❀❀❀

Myths hold a society together. When a society begins laughing at its myths, a revolution may be expected.

◦❀❀❀

Myths endure where notable people cause others to dream, "I, too, want to be like that."

◦❀❀❀

Ideas, not circumstances, shape human beings.

A dream counts for much in state-building.

Those who create ideas govern the state.

You can put a stop to an idea only by means of another idea, not by killing the thinker.

An idea can overthrow a regime.

A society where ideas fetch a high price can compete in the world.

Ideas should be counted among a country's exports.

The state with the more powerful idea prevails.

A stable government embodies an idea that is shared by the nation.

God governs the world. Politicians pretend they do.

◦◦◦◦

When there are at least two political parties, God can get the state to do something. When there is only one party, someone is pretending to be God.

◦◦◦◦

Politicians are no worse than the nation, provided an opposition is allowed to organize.

◦◦◦◦

A politician is no worse than the electorate; being in power just strips him naked.

◦◦◦◦

When you revile politicians you get worse politicians.

◦◦◦◦

The opposition upholds morality while the party in power gets things done. When the party in power thinks it is God, the two parties change places.

◦◦◦◦

In Latvia people believe Satan, not God, governs the world. That is why they dislike politicians.

◦◦◦◦

A politician may have the power to rule human beings, but human beings do not have the power to rule the world.

ᗖᗖᗖᗖ

A person with real power usually keeps quiet and acts. People who think they rule the world are always chattering.

ᗖᗖᗖᗖ

A person with real power never shouts.

ᗖᗖᗖᗖ

Real power is tolerant.

ᗖᗖᗖᗖ

If you use your power to slap someone in the face, your power vanishes.

ᗖᗖᗖᗖ

Either spiritual power is delegated by God or it does not last long.

ᗖᗖᗖᗖ

A nation is a group of people who venerate the same icon.

ᗖᗖᗖᗖ

Every ideology is a set of icons.

ᗖᗖᗖᗖ

Either patriotism is spiritual, or it is a kind of disorderly conduct.

ର ର ର ର

Patriotism should not be a religion.

ର ର ର ର

Reverence for the flag should not go beyond the point where antipathy for other flags begins.

ର ର ର ର

Patriotism should not contradict tolerance.

ର ର ର ର

Patriotism is love for one's own little world. It should not be allowed to break the big world into pieces.

ର ର ର ର

One should travel now and then because home creates habit, and something may seem good which is not so good.

ର ର ର ର

People who never leave home begin to worship themselves.

ର ର ର ର

A people that claims to have its own God has its own idol.

ର ର ର ର

History hands down national myths. People can be the sacrificial victims of their own history.

◌◌◌◌

If God stands behind authority, those who oppose it look unattractive.

◌◌◌◌

The best defense is to have God on your side, but this works only if you obey God.

◌◌◌◌

In God's war there are not innocent victims.

◌◌◌◌

When God enters a fight, the weaker side wins.

◌◌◌◌

The trouble with victory is that there is a loser.

◌◌◌◌

A day of victory is a night.

◌◌◌◌

War is a failure of imagination in two states at the same time.

◌◌◌◌

A material goal never brings peace.

◌◌◌◌

You cannot impose paradise by force.

✺✺✺

If you try to force a beautiful dream upon the world, the world will respond with cynical anecdotes.

✺✺✺

Socialism is based on a dream that is destined to remain a dream.

✺✺✺

Socialism is a foolish dream. Capitalism should not dare to exist without a dream.

✺✺✺

Communism is a fool's dream. Capitalism is a wise man's dream of money.

✺✺✺

Only a spiritual capitalism can defeat Communism.

✺✺✺

A Communist who fought for equality grew old and died. In heaven he was very upset.
"There is no justice here," he said. "Here one person gets one thing and the next person gets something else."
"On the contrary," God replied, "there is true justice only here. Each human being is made for something different. That is why it is unjust to give everybody the same thing."

Capitalism is an elemental force; socialism is the hopeless attempt to make plans without taking God's presence into account.

Capitalism is the world on its own.

A Communist died and came before God.
"Where is Communism?" he asked God.
"Out there!" God replied, pointing to the exit from paradise.

Revolutions take us backwards.

Progress does not mean striving for tomorrow but learning from yesterday.

Progress does not exist, only the discovery of one and the same truth over and over again.

We should not try to build paradise on earth. Paradise is the place for paradise.

A state needs a living idea to hold it together. Money cannot unite a state.

The dictatorship of money means the approach of a revolution.

A state is in good order when its soul, not its finances, is in good order.

When living for money replaces the life of the soul, the soul turns traitor.

It is difficult to market noble principles.

When it comes to scandals, at least, Latvia is not provincial.

If the poor hate the rich because of their money, they are as avaricious as the rich. Property is good for the body, but avarice is bad for the soul.

ᴓᴓᴓᴓ

If the state does not contribute to spirituality, its citizens become disloyal.

ᴓᴓᴓᴓ

If you put too much emphasis on money in your life, in heaven you will feel the bite of poverty.

ᴓᴓᴓᴓ

A heap of money does not make a good grave marker. In heaven you ponder the penny you gave the beggar, not your bank balance.

ᴓᴓᴓᴓ

Religion helps you endure inequality of wealth.

ᴓᴓᴓᴓ

Someone was living in relative poverty and feeling bad about it. He saved as much as he could and threw out nothing of value.

One day Jesus came to see him and said, "Dear friend, I want to help you get rich."

"What do I have to do?" the man asked.

"Just say once, 'Come into my life, God, and solve my money problems.'"

The man spoke the words but they did not seem to have any effect. A bit later, though, he began to notice how many useless things he had in his house. He began going through them and in the end he threw them all out. Even without additional income, he started feeling better.

"It looks as if I was not as bad off as I thought," the man said to Jesus.

"Just wait," Jesus replied. "You've only been at it for a day."

∕∂∂∂∂

God answers your prayer for money by giving you the opportunity to earn it.

∕∂∂∂∂

An economy is healthy when everyone is working; it is weak when everyone is waiting for it to get better.

∕∂∂∂∂

Money is a number; the soul is infinity.

∕∂∂∂∂

Money loves only itself.

∕∂∂∂∂

Money does not understand itself.

∕∂∂∂∂

God and money cannot be combined, but they can coexist.

∕∂∂∂∂

A child grows up the minute you give him money.

ᵒᵒᵒᵒ

Only in childhood and on Sundays can we take no account of time or money.

ᵒᵒᵒᵒ

A wealthy country is a place where people think about God a lot, not a place where you can buy lots of things.

ᵒᵒᵒᵒ

There was once a golden calf who played the role of God. Many people believed in him, but the heavens were displeased. "You should try to understand the heavens," God told him. The golden calf tried and tried and tried— and finally turned into a cloud.

ᵒᵒᵒᵒ

A young man broke into the highest heaven. Everyone there was talking about God, while he talked only about money. Everyone laughed at him. He was the court jester of paradise.

ᵒᵒᵒᵒ

The world cannot put itself in order by itself.

ᵒᵒᵒᵒ

In God's plans there is always room for God.

8

Culture

There was an artist who lived in a small city on the edge of Europe. He often dreamed about Paris.

"How I would like to go there and live among all the famous artists," he thought.

One day Jesus dropped in. "I'd like to take you with me to Paris," he said.

"Are you an artist, too?" the young man asked.

"To a certain extent, yes," Jesus answered. "There's something I want to paint."

"What do you want to paint?" the artist asked.

"I want to paint a picture of the unseen world that exists right next to you. You'll see it if you just pay attention," Jesus answered.

☞

Poetry is submission to the truth that the world is a mystery to us.

☞

Dreams arise from the fact that reality is God's dreams, not mine.

☞

When dreams meet matter, an awakening occurs that you cannot blame on matter.

At least half of all books are about God, although they avoid the word. The other half are about the authors themselves.

Human beings want to create a world of their own because they are created in the image and likeness of the One who created the world.

Ideals arise from deficiencies.

Art is a defense against bare walls. Bare souls do not like bare walls.

A painting is a dream on the wall.

A painting is concretized spirit.

Art is the canonization of a dream.

Art depicts either a truth about the nature of the world or a dream about the nature of God.

116

❦

Given a painting of a naked cherub and an icon of a gloomy divine face, people usually fail to believe that the former is truer.

❦

Infinity does not evoke an emotional response, so God created icons.

❦

Good taste cannot substitute for ideas in art.

❦

The artist's tool is not just the brush but the soul.

❦

Art is the truth about the soul and the spirit that inhabits it.

❦

Sacred art is idolatry within normal limits.

❦

Sacred art flourishes in periods when there are no prophets. Prophets struggle against sacred art.

❦

Saints are the opposite of sacred art.

❦

Sacred art, if God guides it, arrives at symbols of God which it cannot understand, at which point sacred art becomes just art again.

❦

From secular art it is possible to arrive at sacred art, at which point you understand that the whole world is an icon.

❦

When a religion is dying it becomes art.

❦

Faith in sacred art is the end of religion.

❦

Sacred art does not save, but its opposite is emptiness and atheism.

❦

There is no new art, just period art.

❦

The world has the capacity to depict beauty but not to be beautiful.

❦

An accurate portrait is not the one you want to hang on the wall.

❦

Dreams must not be realized if they are to remain beautiful.

❦

The world is small and dear to us. Truth is vast. That's why we have fairy tales.

❦

Jesus said to his Father: "The question of what a creature should know about God is so complicated that we need to investigate it by making new creatures and new civilizations. I cannot say for sure what a creature should or should not know."

❦

A historical period is a new idea.

❦

The limitedness of thought produces historical periods. Dogma is the result of the limitedness of thought.

❦

Great ages leave pyramids behind. Minor ages take pride in a penny saved.

❦

Great ages leave behind tourist destinations for minor ages.

119

❦

Historical periods leave ideas behind; the people are secondary.

❦

Periods pass, pyramids remain.

❦

Culture is created by thinkers who find a modus vivendi for the soul in a certain place.

❦

The dreams of an age come from not wanting to look at its filth.

❦

Either a culture is sustained by some sort of theological question or it disappears.

❦

Happy ages are religious.

❦

Civilizations go to ruin when there are too many kinds of desserts.

❦

Civilization begins with ideas and persons; it ends with sex and war.

❦

The people who shape a historical period do not sense when it is over.

❦

The death of a myth is the beginning of the death of a civilization.

❦

When a culture begins ironizing about itself it has begun its decline.

❦

Irony ruins myths.

❦

Joy is not wise. It is sadness that is wise.

❦

We use irony to shield ourselves from wisdom; there is no such defense against foolishness.

❦

Culture begins with holiness and ends with irony.

❦

Jokes have two endings—one in heaven,
the other in hell.

❦

Jokes do not come from love; there is always something they do not love.

❦

In Eden an angel said, "Ridicule is the opposite of love."
"What do you mean by that?" the others asked.
"Love loves what ridicule makes fun of," the angel replied.

❦

Adam asked God, "Does ridicule have any place in the life of the Trinity?"
"Sometimes," God replied. "Now and then we say to each other, 'You are just like Adam!' That stops the conversation and we have to laugh."

❦

The world often laughs at itself because it does not want to be God.

❦

Jokes justify the world.

❦

Humor is the process of natural selection for wisdom.

❦

Wit is wisdom smiling.

✆

Humor is looking at yourself from behind.

✆

There were two clowns in a circus. One of them threw pies in the other's face. The audience laughed. When the act was over, the clowns went behind the curtains. "Why does everyone laugh when you throw a pie in my face?" one clown asked the other.
"Because they are not wise enough to explain it," the other replied.

✆

A professor was talking with his neighbor the clown.
"I study the stars," he was saying, "and each day I get wiser."
"I make stupid jokes," the clown replied, "and each day I get wiser by not laughing at them myself."

✆

A professor was talking with his neighbor the clown.
"The world is a joke we are not permitted to laugh at," the professor said.
"Not unless you want the joke to be on you," the clown added.

✆

A professor was talking with his neighbor the clown.
"The world is the wisest thing God has made," the professor said.

The clown disagreed. "The wisest thing God has made is a clown with his feet in the air."

"I don't understand," the professor said.

"Jokes are wisdom with its feet in the air. If you turn a joke upside down, it turns into wisdom again."

☞

Do not make your jokes too wise if you want to be happy.

☞

Wisdom should not be immoderate. Immoderate wisdom is a joke to the angels.

☞

A new angel appeared in Eden. All he could do was make jokes.

"God must want us to smile," the angels concluded.

"No, God just wants to keep your wisdom from destroying you," the new angel said.

"You mean, wisdom can destroy us?" the angels asked.

"Yes, if it is not joined with love," God replied.

☞

What you can make jokes about does not last long.

☞

Humor is a response to the evil in human beings.

❧

The world holds fast to what it does not make fun of.

❧

Worlds come to an end when they become preoccupied with themselves.

❧

Large nations tend to focus on themselves; small nations have to be cosmopolitan if they do not want their spiritual life to be utterly insignificant.

❧

The provinces are for poets, not politicians.

❧

There was a city named Riga where many church steeples were topped with weathercocks, not crosses. "I hope this city will wake up some day," God sighed as he watched the trams making their daily rounds.

A PLACE WHERE
I WAS ALONE
WITH GOD.
THERE I SAW STRANGE
LANDSCAPES THAT
NO ONE HAD SEEN
BEFORE.

9

Spiritual Life

There was a shopping mall in what was once an airplane hangar. The hangar felt its life had become too mundane. "Nothing but buying and selling goes on under my roof nowadays," the hangar complained to God. "No one thinks about navigating the heavens."

"People can find the heavens under your roof, too," God told the hangar. "They just have to look up."

"All they will see is a ceiling," said the hangar.

"Flyers who see only clouds in the heavens are no better," God replied.

~

There was a little clay statue of the Buddha. It had been purchased in India by a tourist who had traded a bottle of perfume for it. Both the buyer and the seller had haggled and deceived each other. The statue had bad karma.

One day Jesus decided to rescue the statue. "Let this little statue turn into nothing," he said.

The Buddha's statue smiled. It knew it would attain nirvana. Absolute nothingness and liberation from all suffering. For a brief moment the statue was at peace. Then suddenly it realized, "I am a little statue of the Buddha. I represent the Buddha. I feel something. Is there no nirvana?"

"There is no nirvana," Jesus said, and he smiled.
The little statue began to think. It was thinking about
the Zen koan, "There is no nirvana."

~

There was a young man who venerated the Buddha
and kept a little statue of the Buddha in his apartment.
But in a moment of anxiety he turned to Jesus. Jesus
received him, and the two became the best of friends.
But the young man suffered pangs of conscience. He
had betrayed his first spiritual teacher.
"Who is the Buddha?" Jesus asked him.
"There is no Buddha," the young man replied sadly.
"You have not answered the question correctly," Jesus
said. And he asked again, "Who is the Buddha?"
"The Buddha was a man who thought about how to
liberate the world from suffering," the young Buddhist
answered.
"That is correct," Jesus replied. "I, too, have given
this matter some thought, but the task cannot be
accomplished as long as love exists. Love leads to
attachment. Attachment leads to suffering. I, too, was
attached—to my heavenly Father. That brought me a lot
of suffering, but I have never regretted that suffering."

~

There was a little statue of the Buddha.
"Who is the Buddha?" God asked the statue one day.
"I am the Buddha," the little statue replied.

"What was there before you?" God asked.

"Just some clay," the little statue replied.

"You are not the Buddha," God said.

"I know," the little statue replied.

"What is it you know?" God asked.

"That I am only clay. I am made of components that will come apart one day."

"What will be left over?" God asked.

"I don't know, I am not the Buddha," the little statue said.

"Who is the Buddha?" God asked again.

"A human being who understands what I do not understand," the little statue said.

"What is a human being?" God asked.

"Something made of components that will come apart one day," the little statue said.

"You are wrong," God replied. "A human being is what is left over."

~

Spirit and the spiritual are found in the world, not in emptiness.

~

The soul needs the world, not emptiness.

~

You meet God in the world. In emptiness you meet yourself.

129

~

"What is God?" the Buddha asked.
"An endless koan," God replied in the voice of Jesus.

~

There was a fervent believer who thought about God
from morning to night. One night God appeared to
him in a dream and said, "Dear friend, why have you
forgotten me?"
"What do you mean?" the man asked. "All my life I've
thought of nothing but you."
"That's fine," God said, "but I also want you to
recognize me."

~

Someone became friends with God.
"You'll have a hard life," God said.
"Why?" the person asked.
"Because I will want to give you all that I can," God
replied, "and that is a problem because I can give you
everything."

~

Spirituality is the knowledge that spirit exists, not just
refinement and good taste.

~

When the soul devotes itself fully to its relationship
with God, God gives it as much as it is capable of

receiving at each moment. Hence spiritual growth proceeds in a calm and measured way.

~

A soul can receive as much as it can believe.

~

There is no soul which cannot come to Christ, but each person's path is different.

~

Every soul has something of Judas in it. Every soul has something of John in it.

~

In every Christian there is a bit of Jesus.

~

All paths lead to Jesus.

~

No one is worthy of Jesus' holiness.
No one is unworthy of Jesus' holiness.

~

The cross is obedience to God's will.
Only the way of the cross leads to heaven.
There is no other way.

∽

God knows human beings well and therefore does not tell them everything.

∽

God knows human beings well and creates an earthly life that is not easy for them.

∽

Golgotha means dying obediently.
The way of the cross means living obediently.

∽

No way is more beautiful than the way of the cross.
Only those who walk in it understand this.

∽

The way of the cross ends in heaven.

∽

Everyone has a personal Gethsemane.
Everyone has a personal Bethlehem.
Everyone has a personal Nazareth.
Everyone has a personal Jerusalem.
The cross of the Son of God belongs to the Son of God alone.
There is only one Son of God.
The children of God are those who want to be.
The heavenly Jerusalem begins on earth.

~

Life with God is interesting.
Life with God is not easy on earth.
Life with God is easy in heaven.
We can make sense of life on earth only if we keep
heaven in mind.

~

There is no such thing as a completely healthy soul.
People who pretend to be better than they are, are
trying to deceive God.

~

A person who lives the life of the soul is in paradise
already on earth.

~

There is a large measure of pride in asceticism.
Obedience pleases God most. An average person who is
obedient can outrank a monk.

~

Monks have their own tasks. They are not better than
other people. Monks are necessary, but not everyone
can be a monk. Monks are called to serve those who
are not monks. The cloister is a special form of service,
not meant for everyone. Every soul has its own form of
service. God personally chooses souls for the cloister.

∾

Every soul has its place.
Every soul has a place with God.

∾

Souls feel at home in God.

∾

Human beings do not have to seek the will of God.
The will of God is right beside them.
The will of God is in them if they seek God.

∾

You cannot earn a childlike soul.
You cannot construct a childlike soul.
You can pray for a childlike soul.
Pray for it!

∾

The intimation that God exists transforms a person.

∾

God is the one and only terminal point of spiritual
quests.

∾

A body without a soul is a corpse. So is a soul without
God.

~

When a soul soars too high, it experiences its own lowliness, not God's loftiness.

~

A soul which has experienced God will always be lonely in the company of others because there is no second God.

~

The world is the moment, the soul is eternity.

~

To overcome your fear of infinity, you need to believe that God was born on Christmas Day.

~

The soul should not say to itself "I am not God," but "I want to be an icon."

~

You cannot make a profit from spirituality because God is too costly.

~

There are financial centers and spiritual centers. In financial centers people buy spirituality. In spiritual centers they give it away for free.

❧

God does not try to frighten the obedient.

❧

The culture of eternity is ascetical because human nature is flawed.

❧

God demands obedience, not a complicated theology.

❧

Spirituality becomes fanatical if even one percent of it is idolatrous.

❧

If you put too much emphasis on sex and delicatessens in your life, in heaven you will suffer from loneliness and hunger.

❧

The world becomes peaceful when it senses the image of God within it.

❧

There was a seagull that loved to fly over the sea and view the waves. In the fall the wind was too strong and the gull had to take shelter behind the pine dunes. It was not as beautiful there, but you could still sense the presence of something grand beyond the trees.

"I don't want to live without the sea," the gull told God.
"You should learn how to feel the sea breeze even when
you are flying over a city," God replied.

~

There was a bathhouse where people changed when
they went swimming. One day a seagull landed there.
"What a dull life you have!" the gull said to the
bathhouse. "All you can do is stand here and look at the
sea. I can fly over it."
"You don't understand me," the bathhouse replied. "I
offer people privacy, and I don't tell anyone what I see."
"What is so interesting about that?" the gull asked.
"I'm not going to tell you," the bathhouse replied.

~

In Eden an angel said, "Adam loves to talk about
his inner life. It seems to be as interesting to him as
everything else in the world put together."

~

A confessional booth once said to God, "I know a
great deal."
"So do I," God smiled.

~

A clown came home from work feeling tired and sad.
"Why do I always feel so sad after a performance?" he
asked God.

Hearing no answer, he went to bed. In a dream he saw an angel who told him, "I have come to cheer you up. Your work is very difficult. You have to laugh even when you don't feel like it. So your soul wants to relax by feeling sad."

~

Why is it not possible to see God? Because this world is designed to prepare human beings gradually for a world where they will see God whether they want to or not.

~

There was an old radio that nobody turned on anymore. "It is difficult for me to be quiet all the time," the radio said to God.
"Be quiet along with me," God replied.

~

The most beautiful music of all is silence in God's company.

~

There was once an ordinary, gray winter day.
"Nothing ever happens on me," the day complained. "Just countless snowflakes falling, one after the other, and countless people going about their business. Everything is as usual. An ordinary day."

~

There was a person who loved nature very much.
Whenever he had any problems, he took a walk in the
forest. There all sorts of ideas occurred to him and
problems got solved. He lived a long life and died.
"Why did you never go to church?" God asked him.
"I liked it better in the forest," the person answered.
"I wanted you also to know the one whose voice you
heard in the forest," God told him.

~

After God's Sunday comes God's Monday.

~

Only for the person who sets himself up as God is God
not there.

~

The people who receive the most are those who let God
give them what God wants to give them.

~

The minute you decide you no longer need God, you
discover the world no longer needs you.

~

A hard life is beautiful.

God created me. God knows why.

God can see everything. Happiness is God watching you.

To fight against God is to fight against yourself.

Obeying God means obeying one who wills more good for you than you will for yourself.

Confessing your faults to God is a way of getting to know yourself and God at the same time.

With God as your traveling companion you see paradise from a tram window.

The family is holy if there is room for God in it.

True beauty looks unlovely.

There is no way back from God.

~

Running into God is not running into a blind alley.

~

It was fall. Cold, wet, and unpleasant.
"Why did you create such a season?" people asked God.
"So that you would come to see its beauty," God replied.
"What's beautiful about rain all day long?" the people asked sullenly.
"This is the season when I want you to think about the things that will make you forget that it is cold and wet outside."

~

There was a wise monk who liked sweets.
"You are not worthy of God," said the abbot.
"I am God's sweet," the monk replied with a smile.

~

There was a wise monk who liked girls.
"You would do better to look at the flowers," God said.
"Ah yes, the flowers," sighed the monk, and he obediently studied the flowers.

~

One day someone caught sight of God.
"It's God!" the person exclaimed.
"Let's be friends," God proposed.

❧

In Eden an angel said, "A creature that obeys God will experience unpleasant as well as pleasant feelings because God is not a creature."

❧

God and a dwarf occasionally played chess. The dwarf always lost, but he still enjoyed it. "Losing to God is a good thing," he said. "Beating God means going down to defeat yourself."

❧

In Eden an angel said, "God is holy because I am bad."
"Explain that!" the others demanded.
"Holiness is endless tolerance," the angel said.

❧

A young person surrendered his free will to God.
"Now your desires will be fulfilled," God told him.
"I don't understand," the youth said.
"By surrendering you unite my will with yours," God explained.

❧

A soul which fully surrenders to God's power does not lose its freedom even for a moment and does nothing which is unacceptable to itself.

When you let God steer your life, you become freer than when you steer it by yourself. The control of the living God does not in any way limit a person. When you let God live through you, you do not know how much of your activity comes from yourself and how much comes from God; you only know that there is something of God there. You are not interested in knowing how much, for you do not pretend to be God.

A person who gives God absolute control of his life becomes as free as God. God is human.

There is clock time and soul time. They rarely coincide.

To be vain is to be blind.

A creature will never attain the perfection of God; therefore its conduct will never be so virtuous that God's laws for its life will be unnecessary.

A creature's will is God-given, so the creature should not regard it as the only will that exists.

~

A creature cannot break itself in two. Its behavior will always be half-right.

~

A creature's holiness is always connected with an awareness of its own insignificance; otherwise it is not holiness but simply ignorance of God.

~

A creature's idea of what is right will always be limited.

~

When a creature takes no interest in God, it has only other creatures to compare itself to.

~

You can deny your nature only up to a point; otherwise even your feelings for God melt away. Knowing God demands self-denial, not self-destruction.

~

Trusting in God helps you improve yourself; knowing how the world is put together is neutral.

~

No one can comfort a creature the way God can.

~

To hear God you have to pay attention to God.

~

God's will for human beings is more human than their own.

~

When a soul lets Jesus dwell in it, it should not ask what Jesus would do but what it should do so that Jesus can dwell in it. The soul will never fully understand how God lives through human beings, for God's mind is greater than the human mind. A life like this is a continuous, beautiful mystery of trust in the goodness of God.

~

The humbler a soul is, the more knowledge of God it can bear. The more a soul knows about God, the humbler it becomes.

~

The souls of people who let God into their lives are shaped by the divine and human natures—a free person and a free God. Such a situation liberates people from every picture of God they might have except for Jesus, the person who from birth was one with God.

~

Obedience to God guarantees my freedom.

~

God asked Adam, "What is it that you are thinking about me?"

145

Adam replied, "That you are three, yet one. I do not understand it."
"You never will, but thinking about it is not a sin."

～

A wise monk was thinking about the Trinity.
"Don't think so much," God told him. "Just be like Jesus."

～

There was a wise monk. He knew the secret of the Trinity and died of its beauty.

～

Someone asked God, "What does the Trinity mean?"
"It means I have my own inner life," God replied.

～

When you cross paths with God you run into happiness.

～

"It's all over!" That is the feeling when God shows up unexpectedly.

～

A man of advanced years decided the time had come to think about eternity, for his life was drawing to a close.
"It's time to start thinking more about God," he said to himself. "But how do I go about it?"
He thought and thought but could not come up with an answer.

Suddenly he wondered, "Perhaps I should just ask God?"
"I am surprised you found the answer so quickly," God
complimented him.

~

An actor was trying to play God. "I am all-powerful!" he
said, and he stumbled. God did not say anything.
The actor tried again. "I am all-powerful!" he said, and
this time he did not stumble. God did not say anything.
"I am God!" the actor said.
"Then let's be friends," God offered.

~

God is not a vehicle. Do not try to steer God.

~

Do not do to God what you would not do to yourself.

~

A person wanted to be friends with the heavens.
"We are very big," the heavens told him.
"But I'm lonely, I don't have a friend," the person replied.
"We want to be your friend," the heavens answered,
"but you also need someone who is as small as you."

THE SPACE BETWEEN
TWO PEOPLE

10

Love

"How should we make Adam and Eve?" God asked.
"We want them to love each other, but we do not want
them to forget us. Let us do it this way: When Adam
loves God, he will see how beautiful Eve is. When he
focuses on Eve alone, something will be missing. When
Eve looks for our image in Adam, she will find Adam
attractive. When she does not, she will see only Adam's
shortcomings."
Thus God spoke, and it came to pass.

A girl paid a visit to her boyfriend. "I love you very
much," she told her friend. "I want to be yours."
"Come here," her friend said. "I was really hoping you
would visit."
They spent the night together and in the morning the
girl went home.
"I want to be that boy's wife," she said to God.
"It's not going to happen," God replied.
"Why not?" the girl asked. She did not understand.
"I have other plans for you," God told her.
"You don't like us being together?" the girl asked.
"I don't like the fact that there is no room for me
between you," God replied.

꩜

A young woman liked a young man, but the pair did not have an opportunity to get better acquainted. They lived out their lives and died. In paradise they saw each other again.

"Why did nothing come of our love on earth?" the woman asked God.

"Because that man's love for you was heavenly," God replied.

꩜

There was a married couple. He was a poet, she was an artist. They did not have much money, but they got by. They lived in peace and harmony. Do you know why? Because one of them once said to God, "God, shape this marriage however you please."

꩜

To love is to understand that I am who I am, you are who you are, and God exists.

꩜

Love consists of sex, ideas, and eternity.

꩜

A loving fool is wiser than the angels.

꩜

You do not have to love correctly, you just have to love.

෧

Love governs the world.
Jesus judges the world.
Jesus is love.

෧

Love is linked to suffering.
Suffering purifies.
Love heals.
Life is beautiful.
Life is short.
Paradise is eternal.

෧

Suffering love rescues the loveless soul.

෧

Love is delight in the existence of another person.
Delight in the beauty of another passes quickly.

෧

To love is to want another person to acknowledge that
it was worth creating you.

෧

In the presence of beauty you will always be unlovely. If
you wish to feel beautiful, you must look for something
less lovely than yourself.

☙

Divinity manifests itself by loving what is not divine.

☙

It is not difficult to love good people. It is difficult to love people as they are.

☙

Love created the world. We get to know the world by loving it.

☙

Love shrinks the dimensions of the world.

☙

Love cannot have come from the Big Bang.

☙

God's "mistake" is the mystery of love.

☙

To love is to love deficiencies, not perfection. Love of perfection is non-acceptance of the world.

☙

Love tolerates the world; perfection does not.

☙

Perfection and love are opposites.

❧

Love and forgiveness are one and the same.

❧

Loving nothing but perfection is evil. Goodness means loving evil.

❧

Love gives us the right to be unlovely.

❧

Love is the beauty of the unlovely.

❧

God's love is something like a fig leaf.

❧

In every person there is a constant struggle between love and the beast.

❧

Sex cannot be eternal; love at a distance can be eternal.

❧

If sex is the only thing you dream about, eternity is unbearable.

❧

Sex lasts a minute. Knowing yourself and the other is lasting.

↻

Erotic love must develop into a spiritual bond if you wish to sit next to your beloved in heaven.

↻

Sex ends at the grave; theology, in heaven.

↻

Adam said to God, "I love Eve. Isn't that wrong, since you told me that I should love you alone?"
"It is not wrong as long as you do not forget that I am in the midst of you," God replied.

↻

"You have experienced the Song of Songs," God told somebody.
"I don't understand," the person said.
"You live in unfulfilled love," God replied.

↻

The person who does not know how to suffer does not know how to love.

↻

Love does not commit adultery.

↻

Love is without limits, morality is not.

❧

Love is stronger than strength.

❧

God's love has no limits; a creature's capacity to understand it does.

❧

The only logical proof of God's love is: you do not deserve to exist, yet you do.

❧

God takes pleasure even in those who do not take pleasure in God.

❧

A strong person does not give us a good picture of God because God loves those who are weaker than God. A beautiful person does not give us a good picture of God because God loves those who are not as beautiful as God. People who need love give us a good picture of God.

❧

God created something. There was absolutely nothing special about that something.
"Why on earth is something like this needed?" the angels asked.
"For the same reason the world is needed," God replied.
"We do not understand," the angels said.

"The world is nothing in my presence, but I love it," God said.

☙

An angel said, "Being in God's presence means being in the presence of someone infinitely holy who never reproaches creation for not being God."

☙

Everything is inferior to God, so God's love is never deserved.

☙

If you can say "I deserve God's love," you really mean "I am better than God."

☙

If God's love were forfeited because of sin, God could only love God.

☙

When a creature understands the love of God, its own insignificance does not frighten it.

☙

Only God can endure the unholiness of the world and still rejoice over the world as if it were the holiest of the angels.

꩜

A creature loves something better than itself; only God can love a nullity.

꩜

"What is benevolence?" an angel asked God.
"Love of the wicked," God replied.
"How can that be—they are wicked!" the angel exclaimed.
"Benevolence loves something other than itself," God said.

꩜

Evil cannot understand benevolence, nor benevolence evil; but together they sense something higher than themselves.

꩜

Transgressing God's law means making trouble for yourself, not losing God's love.

꩜

The inner life of God is the love of three divine persons for each other and for everything else.

꩜

Love is not symmetrical.

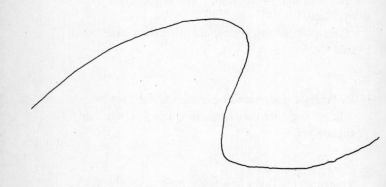

A BEAUTIFUL, PLEASANT
AND PAINFUL WAVE

11
The Mystery of Good and Evil

"Could there not be something good in the world?" God asked. "Let us try to create it."

So God willed, and Something Good came into being.

"I am good," said Something Good. "What are you?"

"I am holy," God replied.

"The holy is not the good?" Something Good asked.

"They are different, but it is not easy to explain," God said.

"So you must be bad?" Something Good asked.

"I am not bad, either," God replied.

"But you are not good?" Something Good persisted.

"I am holy," God explained again. "It is not easy to understand."

"But if something is not good, it must be bad," Something Good said.

"In principle, yes," God agreed, "but I am not bad."

"And you are not good, either?" Something Good replied.

"I am holy," God said again.

"In other words, bad," Something Good concluded.

"There is something besides good and bad," God said.

"For sure—something totally bad!" Something Good concluded. "And that is what you must be!"

God sighed and changed Something Good into something else.

Ↄ

A person was on friendly terms with the angels. One day the angel Satan dropped in.

"I would like to make your acquaintance," Satan said. The person listened carefully.

"I am not some kind of mindless evil that God tolerates without our knowing why," the angel explained. "I stand for something else."

"For what?" the person asked.

"Your need for sex, for example, or your taste for meat, or your right to be without being God," the angel replied. As the person listened, God broke into the conversation.

"Satan is my friend," God said, "but being friends with him is tricky. Satan is my opposite. Everything Satan stands for must be held in check if you want to be happy."

"This liberation through repression is illusory," Satan observed. "You cannot destroy the satanic element in human beings or creation without destroying creation itself."

"True," God replied, "but it should not be the ruling element. Otherwise, you are the captive of your own created nature."

Ↄ

Someone died in a plague.

"Why did you create a world in which there are all sorts of illnesses that spoil a person's life?" the victim scolded God.

"So that you would understand that something that only causes problems also has a right to exist. If the world were perfect according to your view of things, you would soon fail to understand why you yourself are permitted to exist," God replied.

☉

A good destiny and an evil destiny ran into each other one day.
"Who are you?" the evil one asked the good.
"I am a good destiny," it replied. "And you?"
"I am an evil destiny," the other said.
At that point the two of them happened to look down at a puddle in the road, and they discovered that they were identical.
"Impossible!" they cried out.
God said, "You have to understand that when people flee their destiny, it is evil; when they go out to meet it, it is good."

☉

There is good, there is evil, and there is God.

☉

The world is prone to evil, but evil is complex. Real evil is done by those who think it is good.

☉

Evil people think they are good, but their ideas of good and evil are wrong.

〲

The world is not-God, not something evil.

〲

Evil is the incompleteness of the world.

〲

Evil is evil only as the created mind understands it. God alone knows the truth about it.

〲

Evil does not love evil.

〲

Evil does not love itself.

〲

Evil can never be happy.

〲

Evil finds solace in irony.

〲

Seeking to justify itself, evil arrives at the idea of good.

〲

When it laughs at itself, evil recognizes that it is permitted to exist.

꙰

Evil wants a relationship with good, not evil.

꙰

Evil looks for love because love will not destroy it.

꙰

The world loves those who do not judge evil because the world itself is not good.

꙰

Adam's world will destroy itself if it is governed by the dogma of the struggle between good and evil rather than the idea of the non-destruction of evil.

꙰

Dreaming of annihilating evil amounts to imagining that the world does not exist.

꙰

True good and true evil have to do with God's view of things. The world has only its dreams.

꙰

Creation does not believe that God is good because it takes itself as the criterion.

꙰

God's will seems evil to people who see themselves as good.

꙳

God looks like a fool to evil.

꙳

The good person and the evil person compare themselves with each other. Neither the good person's view of the evil person nor the evil person's view of the good person is correct.

꙳

There needs to be sadness in the world because the world's pleasures are so shallow.

꙳

Human beings are not naturally good, but they usually do not refuse to take the right path.

꙳

It is interesting to talk with monsters because they have thought about existence, about whether they should exist or not.

꙳

We cannot go on seeing the evil of the world and take pleasure in the illusion "We are better."

꙳

Wisdom does not lie in exposing the evil of the world but in figuring out what to do with it.

ↄ

It is not possible to understand goodness, but it is
possible not to want evil.

ↄ

Wisdom does not understand goodness; it just tells you
that evil is stupid.

ↄ

In the depths lurks the awareness that I am not good.
In the heights there is the awareness that God exists.

ↄ

The world's true nature is transcendent; therefore a
creature cannot say what is good and what is evil.

ↄ

Yes and No together create the world.

ↄ

God's spirit is always a little crooked. Evil loves perfect
outlines.

ↄ

In God's plan there is room for chance.

ↄ

Goodness cannot exist alone.

◌

Goodness and feeling good are different things.

◌

Goodness is loving that which is Not-I.

◌

The mission of goodness is to give itself to evil.

◌

Goodness is non-destruction of evil.

◌

Goodness chooses evil over emptiness because evil shows it what the world actually is.

◌

Goodness defends itself by means of itself.

◌

God created the angel Satan. Satan was very proud. He felt superior to God. But God did not take offense. "Think whatever you like," God said to Satan. "I am still God, and you are just the angel Satan."

◌

God does not like Satan's plans. Neither does Satan.

↻

God actually happens in the world. Satan merely philosophizes.

↻

The world invents Satan when it fails to understand God.

↻

God said to Adam, "I have made a whole world for you where you must live until the splendor of paradise shines again."
"I like it better here in paradise," Adam said. "I do not understand the harsh and unpleasant world you have created."
"It is a beautiful world," God replied. "You just have to get used to it."

↻

An angel said to God: "Why did you create such a terrible world, where countless creatures seek to devour each other?"
"This is the world that was in Adam," God replied. "It is terrible, but it is also capable of seeing God."

↻

An angel had a dream: people desired nothing but the good, and there was no evil at all. "Why is the world so imperfect?" the angel asked God.

"The world is not a second God," God replied. "The world exists to see God."

꩜

One morning Adam did not feel well.
"Who invented all these illnesses?" he asked God.
"Illnesses help you," God replied.
"How?" Adam asked in surprise.
"They prevent you from feeling great in God's presence," God said.

꩜

Illness reminds you of what you are.

꩜

God created something good.
"God, too, is good," Something Good declared. "I must be God."
God created something average.
"God is not average," Something Average declared. "I must not be God."
God created something evil.
"God is not evil," Something Evil declared. "How nice!"

꩜

One day a cowboy saw an angel standing before him.
"Who are you?" the cowboy asked, drawing his pistol.
"I am an angel," the angel replied.
"What do you want with me?" the cowboy asked.

"I have been sent to tell you that you ought to go to
church once in a while," the angel said.
"The church people disapprove of me," the cowboy replied.
"People also disapproved of Jesus," the angel noted.
"But Jesus was holy," the cowboy answered.
"Yes, but every person has it in him to be a little like
Jesus," the angel said.

❧

There is no person who is worthy of God. There is no
person who is unworthy of God.

❧

No one suffers undeservedly. Suffering is a gift from God.

❧

A person cannot understand God without suffering.
Only in heaven will we learn why there must be
suffering.

❧

Happiness is understanding the goodness of God, not
the whole of God.

❧

The world is not finished.

❧

Living in the world is beautiful if heaven is at hand.

THE HEAVENS ARE NOT
EMPTY. THE WORLD BEGAN
LONG AGO. "WHAT WILL THE
END BE LIKE?" SOMEONE
ASKS. "BEAUTIFUL," GOD SAYS.

12

The World to Come

A terrible murderer grew old and died.

"Surely I will not see God," he thought. "Only the saints see God."

An angel came to him and said, "Because of all the evil you have done, you must go to a place where there is nobody but God."

"I don't understand," the murderer replied in surprise.

"You are so evil that only God is willing to talk to you," the angel explained.

❧❧❧❧

God's stories do not have happy endings; they end in eternity.

❧❧❧❧

Reaching the boundary we call death, someone said to God, "I am happy my earthly life is over."

"We would advise you to feel a little sorry about it," God said.

"Why?" the person asked.

"Because life in heaven consists of memories of life on earth," God replied.

The destiny of the world is not a happy ending but endless memories.

The end of the world is as interesting as the beginning. The end of one world is the beginning of another.

The Riga canal was once the moat of a fortress, but when the fortifications were torn down it became just a canal. It branches off from the Daugava River, makes a little arc around the city, then rejoins the river.

"Why can't my city be eternal?" the canal asked God one day.

"You do not know what eternity is," God replied to the canal. "Only human beings know that."

"I like human beings very much," the canal said.

"So do I," God replied. "That is why I created them for eternity."

God spreads eternity far and wide.

Eternity is a barrel organ whose one and only tune does not bore you.

Either the thought "I am" is enough for you or you cannot be eternal.

Irony and eternity are opposites.

Adam said to God, "Tell me a bedtime story."
"You are and always will be," God replied. "Sleep in peace."

Paradise plays hide and seek with us while we are alive. It jumps out at us when we are dead.

Someone had a cottage in the heavens. Every morning he took a walk in the clouds, then returned to his cottage.
"Isn't your life monotonous?" someone asked.
"Contemplating the heavens is enough for me," the person replied.

There were two neighbors who disliked each other so much they did not even speak to each other. They died and went to heaven. To their great surprise, God seated them next to each other.

"Why do I have to look at such an ugly face?" they exclaimed together.

"You have all eternity to find something beautiful in that face!" God replied.

∽∂∂∂

One day a cowboy was drinking whisky. A second cowboy came in and picked a fight. In a flash, pistols were drawn and the first cowboy lay dead. The dead cowboy saw a new landscape and an angel drawing near.

"What will become of me?" he asked.

"You will be able to think back over your whole life," the angel replied.

"There was nothing special about it, just some barroom brawls," the cowboy said sadly.

"You have all of eternity to try and see God's image in the people you fought with," said the angel.

∽∂∂∂

A river flowed into the sea.

"Where do I end?" asked the river.

"Nowhere," God replied.

"I don't understand," said the river.

"You don't have to; your job is just to flow before me."

∽∂∂∂

The world creates moments. The soul collects moments for eternity.

୦୦୦୦

Eternity is divided into seven days so that people will not fear infinity.

୦୦୦୦

Human beings create hell on their own initiative. God creates paradise.

୦୦୦୦

Hell is the earth without love.

୦୦୦୦

In the flesh you cannot see God. After death God is everywhere to be seen. If you are not ready for it, paradise can be hell.

୦୦୦୦

Hell is the last merciful gift God grants the godless soul. That is why Satan exists. Hell will last forever.

୦୦୦୦

Hell is an atheist's paradise. You cannot bring God in.

୦୦୦୦

No one who loves goes to hell.

୦୦୦୦

The angel Satan was hostile to human beings and refused to serve them. "You will go to hell," God told him.

175

"If hell exists, then you are not a God of love," Satan replied.

God said, "For you hell will be paradise because you do not obey me."

◦◦◦◦

Jesus asked his Father, "Why is such a terrible place as hell necesssary? Can't people simply repent of their sins?"

The Father answered Jesus, "Those who repent of their sins are not in hell."

"Then who is in hell?" Jesus asked.

"Those who deny God," the Father replied.

"But why do you put them in hell?" Jesus asked.

"Because being any nearer to me would be pure torture for them," God replied.

◦◦◦◦

There was a famous musician. One day he was attacked and killed by a deranged person. The musician came before God.

"You lived a very empty life," God told him, "though I liked your early songs. I kept trying to give you more melodies, but you rarely listened to me."

"What will happen to me?" the musician asked in alarm.

"Your punishment will simply be that what might have been will not be."

ᗞᗞᗞᗞ

Hell is a squandered life.

ᗞᗞᗞᗞ

One day, one cowboy killed another. "One less outlaw in the world!" the victor thought, and he went to the bar for a glass of whiskey.

Meanwhile the dead cowboy saw paradise before him. "You must have made a mistake," he told the angel there. "I am not a good man at all."

"This is the paradise of bad men," the angel explained.

"And what is in it?" asked the cowboy.

"Seats where people do not see each other, but only God," the angel replied.

ᗞᗞᗞᗞ

Sick souls need healing, not punishment.

ᗞᗞᗞᗞ

Cursing God means losing the source of happiness, not courting retribution.

ᗞᗞᗞᗞ

God created Adam. Adam lived a long life, then died. He came before God and said, "Finally I am back in Eden, but everything is very different here."

"So it is," God said. "You made your own paradise while living on earth."

⁄ℴℴℴℴ

You can enter heaven only by way of earth.

⁄ℴℴℴℴ

No one is forced into paradise.

⁄ℴℴℴℴ

People who rely on themselves alone do not reach paradise.

⁄ℴℴℴℴ

On earth no one sees God face to face. In heaven this is granted to those who longed for it on earth.

⁄ℴℴℴℴ

In paradise there is a taste of earth.

⁄ℴℴℴℴ

In eternity the shadow of earth will linger in our souls.

⁄ℴℴℴℴ

People should not ponder why hell and Satan exist, but only what it is like in paradise with God. On earth it is not possible to see what it is like, but sometimes, sensing the presence of God in Christ, you feel a gentle glow.

⁄ℴℴℴℴ

Communion prepares us for paradise.

178

๛๛๛

In paradise we all see what we want.

๛๛๛

Paradise is human.

๛๛๛

Paradise and sweets are different things.

๛๛๛

Paradise is a naive, not a wise place.

๛๛๛

Eternity is pleasant for the soul that takes pleasure in God, not idols.

๛๛๛

You will be able to bear eternity if you focus on God rather than yourself.

๛๛๛

The first paradise was ignorance of certain truths. The second paradise is the conscious overlooking of those truths.

๛๛๛

The boundary of paradise is where wisdom turns into evil.

୭୭୭

The real heaven is in the soul, not somewhere else.

୭୭୭

Paradise is not erotic but theological. Knowing that God exists is more important than a happy marriage.

୭୭୭

Paradise is a place where you see that God is good, not that you are evil.

୭୭୭

Paradise is not talking about your own evil.

୭୭୭

"How do we return to paradise?" It was a question people often asked God.
"Paradise is here already, you just don't see it," God replied. "If you want to know what Adam wanted to know, you will not see paradise. If you want to know what Christ knew, you will be able to see paradise already here on earth."

୭୭୭

A disciple asked Jesus, "Why is life on earth the way it is?"
"So that your paradise will be the way it should be," Jesus replied.

◈◈◈

Paradise is a costly pleasure. You have to pay for it in advance on earth.

◈◈◈

Paradise costs suffering.

◈◈◈

Heaven is everyone's destiny. If you flee from your destiny, you flee from heaven.

◈◈◈

In heaven it is God who moves. The clocks have stopped.

◈◈◈

Heaven is our only home. Everywhere else is a temporary shelter.

◈◈◈

Paradise is wherever God is. If you can discern God in your vicinity, you are living in paradise.

◈◈◈

The most beautiful place in paradise is your own place.

◈◈◈

The beauty of childhood is the landscape of paradise.

ᘓᘓᘓᘓ

Sunday is an image of paradise.

ᘓᘓᘓᘓ

A soul that knows only the ways of the world will be penniless, homeless, and hungry in heaven.

ᘓᘓᘓᘓ

Paradise is just around the corner provided you do not know the future.

ᘓᘓᘓᘓ

Heaven is memories of life on earth.

ᘓᘓᘓᘓ

Heaven exists.

Story of the Temporary World

"What kind of world should I fashion?" God wondered. "I want these fine human beings of mine to live in it and be glad. Everything about it should make them happy."

Thus God spoke and created a wonderful garden for human beings to live in. But they did not behave well. God saw that human beings had a lot to learn.

So God resolved, "I will fashion the world in such a way that they will come to see what they are missing. When they have seen it, I will let them dwell in the beautiful garden again."

"But what shall I do with the world that will no longer be needed? I will make it a temporary world. When human beings have learned their lesson, I will dissolve it and make a new world where they can live and be happy."

Thus God spoke, and so it came to pass.

"We are frightened about the end of the world," the human beings said. "How will it happen?"

"I will command the angels, and they will no longer hold things together in the world as you know it," God said.

"Then what?" the human beings asked.

"There will be another world," God replied.

"What kind of world will that be?" the human beings asked.

"I'll tell you another story!" God said.

Story of the Eternal World

God created human beings. He made a whole world
for them to go to school in. The world fulfilled its
purpose well, and God decided that human beings had
learned all they needed to learn.

"Now it should be possible to put my human beings
back in the wonderful garden. But how can I do it
without frightening them? I will create an invisible
garden right next to them. They will be able to enter it
even though they will not see it. They must get used to
the idea that another world exists right next to the one
in which they went to school."

Thus God decreed and took counsel with the angels
about making an invisible world. The angels advised
setting a deadline for the project. God agreed, and the
work began.

And when is that deadline?

When you realize that a lovely garden exists right
next to you, unseen.

THE RIVER WHERE
THE GARDEN BEGINS

About Paraclete Press

WHO WE ARE

Paraclete Press is an ecumenical publisher of books and recordings on Christian spirituality. Our publishing represents a full expression of Christian belief and practice—from Catholic to Evangelical, from Protestant to Orthodox.

Paraclete Press is the publishing arm of the Community of Jesus, an ecumenical monastic community in the Benedictine tradition. As such, we are uniquely positioned in the marketplace without connection to a large corporation and with informal relationships to many branches and denominations of faith.

We like it best when people buy our books from booksellers, our partners in successfully reaching as wide an audience as possible.

WHAT WE ARE DOING
Books

Paraclete Press publishes books that show the richness and depth of what it means to be Christian. Although Benedictine spirituality is at the heart of all that we do, we publish books that reflect the Christian experience across many cultures, time periods, and houses of worship. We publish books that nourish the vibrant life of the church and its people—books about spiritual practice, formation, history, ideas, and customs.

We have several different series of books within Paraclete Press, including the bestselling Living Library series of modernized classic texts; A Voice from the Monastery—giving voice to men and women monastics about what it means to live a spiritual life today; award-winning literary faith fiction; and books that explore Judaism and Islam and discover how these faiths inform Christian thought and practice.

Recordings

From Gregorian chant to contemporary American choral works, our music recordings celebrate the richness of sacred choral music through the centuries. Paraclete is proud to distribute the recordings of the internationally acclaimed choir Gloriæ Dei Cantores, who have been praised for their "rapt and fathomless spiritual intensity" by *American Record Guide*, and the Gloriæ Dei Cantores Schola, which specializes in the study and performance of Gregorian chant. Paraclete is also the exclusive North American distributor of the recordings of the Monastic Choir of St. Peter's Abbey in Solesmes, France, long considered to be a leading authority on Gregorian chant performance.

Learn more about us at our Web site:
www.paracletepress.com, or call us toll-free at